Women Priests?

9/A32

Women and Religion Series

Forthcoming title:

Women, Theology and the Christian Tradition
Ed. Dr. Janet Martin Soskice

Women Priests?

A Peberdy

Marshall Pickering

Marshall Morgan and Scott
Marshall Pickering
3 Beggarwood Lane, Basingstoke, Hants RG23 7LP, UK

Copyright © 1988 A. Peberdy
First published in 1988 by Marshall Morgan and Scott Publications Ltd
Part of the Marshall Pickering Holdings Group
A subsidiary of the Zondervan Corporation

ISBN: 0 551 01734 1

Text Set in Baskerville by Brian Robinson, Buckingham
Printed in Great Britain by Cox & Wyman, Reading

Contents

Series Introduction   vi
Janet Martin Soskice

The Contributors   vii

Introduction   ix
Alyson Peberdy

1. The Ordination of Women and Anglican-Roman   1
   Catholic Dialogue
   Christopher Hill

2. Would the Symbolism Be All Wrong?   12
   Janet Martin Soskice

3. Priesthood and the Gospel Ministry of Word   22
   and Sacrament
   Philip Holdsworth

4. Women, the Bible and the Priesthood   30
   John and Gillian Muddiman

5. Eucharistic Presidency   49
   John Austin Baker

6. The Way Things Change   61
   Pia Buxton

7. Self-Awareness in the Image of God   70
   Alexina Murphy

Appendix: Open letter to the Bishop of London   78

Series Introduction

Theology, writes the German theologian, J-B Metz, "must again and again be interrupted by praxis and experience. The important questions to be asked by theology, then, are: Who should do theology and where, in whose interest and for whom?"[1]

Women, one assumes, have always been religious, but women have not always written theology. Indeed, if one is considering theology as an academic discipline (certainly not the only definition) then women have only been admitted in any numbers to universities as students of theology since the Second World War.

A remarkable feature of the theological scene in recent years thus has been the steady increase of writings by women on religious matters, and writings about women in religious faith and life. Almost inevitably, many of these writings are by new pens and have appeared in journals of limited circulation. Yet it is sometimes at such edges and not from the heartlands that the faith grows. This series hopes to bring works of importance to wider audiences.

The Women and Religion series has as its broad brief to publish writings of religious importance by women and/or about the place of women in the world's faiths. Some of these writings may recognisably be formal theology, some may not, and some may challenge the distinction of what counts as theology and who is a theologian in the first place.

I am especially grateful to Marshall Pickering for commissioning this series and for their subsequent enthusiasm as it took shape. Special thanks are due, too, to Paul Avis, their editorial advisor, whose idea the series was in the first place and who was relentless in encouraging me to take on its editorship.

[1] J. B. Metz, *Faith in History and Society* (London: Burns & Oates, 1980), p. 58.

Dr Janet Martin Soskice
Ripon College, Cuddesdon

The Contributors

John Austin Baker is Bishop of Salisbury. He has been chairman of the Church of England's Doctrine Commission and of the working party that produced the report *The Church and the Bomb*. His writings include *The Foolishness of God*.

Pia Buxton has been for almost thirty years a member of a Roman Catholic order, the Institute of the Blessed Virgin Mary. After a period as novice mistress in Ascot she moved to York where she became involved in ecumenism and parish renewal. Since 1985 she has been working as a spiritual director in and around Cambridge.

Christopher Hill is a Canon of Canterbury Cathedral and the Archbishop of Canterbury's Secretary for Ecumenical Affairs. In 1983 he became Anglican Secretary to the Anglican-Roman Catholic International Commission.

Philip Holdsworth is a monk of Ampleforth Abbey, who has served on parishes in Warrington, Cheshire, and is now Master of St Benet's Hall, Oxford, a Benedictine house of studies in the University.

Gillian Muddiman teaches Old Testament at St John's College Nottingham and was formerly tutor in Biblical Studies at St Stephen's House, Oxford. Now in deacon's orders she is involved in the life of a local parish as well as pursuing a research degree in Wisdom Christology.

John Muddiman is an Anglican priest and lecturer in New Testament studies at the University of Nottingham. He has been chaplain of New College, Oxford and Vice-Principal of St Stephen's House. Author of *The Bible, Fountain and Well of Truth*, he is a member of the English Anglican-Roman Catholic Commission.

Alexina Murphy is a founder member of the Catholic Women's Network which brings together Roman Catholic women seeking to change their role in the Church. She has been very actively involved in lay ministry in England, Europe and Canada.

Alyson Peberdy trained as a social anthropologist and now works as a Research Fellow at the Open University. Her publications include a study of lay people's responses to women's ministry. She is a member of the General Synod of the Church of England.

Janet Martin Soskice presently lectures at Ripon College, Cuddesdon and will shortly take up a post at Cambridge University as a lecturer in the Faculty of Divinity. She is a Roman Catholic lay woman and author of *Metaphor and Religious Language*.

Introduction

The Roman Catholic Church does not ordain women whilst most Protestant Churches do. Lying between them the Anglican Church, which describes itself as both Catholic and Reformed, is not surprisingly divided over the issue. Along with many other Anglicans (and also Roman Catholics) I find myself asking the reasons for the Catholic practice of restricting ordination to men. Although it contains some interesting leads, classical theology does not provide ready-made answers because the question is generally quite new. But over recent years Vatican statements have put forward a number of reasons and the purpose of these essays is to examine them in detail and to begin to suggest some other ways of looking at this issue.

This is a book for both Roman Catholics and Anglicans and indeed for any who have an interest in the role of women in the Christian churches. On the Anglican side there are essays by the Archbishop of Canterbury's Secretary for Ecumenical Affairs, a bishop and two biblical scholars. The Roman Catholics comprise a lecturer at an Anglican theological college, the Master of a Benedictine house of studies, a lay woman and a nun. Many of the contributors are well-established theologians; men and women drawing upon their academic expertise but writing in a style that is accessible to anyone with an interest in this matter. Between them they tease out the main threads running through the theological arguments in the debate; tradition, symbolism, the Eucharist and eucharistic presidency, Scripture and ecumenism. Then two final essays, one by a nun who works as a spiritual director and the other by a wife and mother, introduce a style and perspective that often tends to be left out.

All of the Roman Catholic contributors to this book regard the ordination of women as a legitimate and fruitful development of Catholic tradition and not, as the Vatican statements suggest, a major departure from the essential elements of the faith. This may come as a surprise to Anglicans, who tend to assume that all Roman Catholics are opposed to women's ordination. But, increasingly, Roman Catholics are discussing and reflecting upon their understanding of priesthood and of the place of women within it. Over the last couple of years here in England a number of Roman Catholic theologians have begun to publically voice their thinking. In 1986 two leading Jesuits lent their signatures to an open letter challenging the Bishop of London's arguments against the ordination of women (see Appendix). Then in March 1987, a conference at Heythrop College, chaired by a Benedictine priest of forty years standing, addressed itself to the question that forms the title of this book. As well as attracting a large number of participants, this meeting received considerable attention from religious and secular national newspapers. The strength of this response clearly indicated that here was an issue of interest and importance to many. And it also became clear that the debate would benefit from Roman Catholics and Anglicans continuing to share their thinking with one another and the church as a whole.

As an Anglican I believe the issues addressed in these essays are of immense practical significance for the Church of England and indeed for the whole Anglican Communion. Back in 1975 the General Synod of the Church of England agreed there were no fundamental objections to the ordination of women but thirteen years on it has still not decided to take the steps that would make it legally possible in England for a bishop to ordain a woman to the priesthood. Meanwhile there have been two major developments. About half of all the other Anglican provinces have decided to go ahead and between them now have well over 1,000 women priests: the Church of England's response has been to pull up the drawbridge with increasing firmness so that no woman priest may be officially allowed to minister in any capacity in England. Then in England itself increasing numbers of women are receiving training for priesthood. One of the main reasons for the reluctance of the Archbishops and General Synod to take the next step is the fear that it would upset Roman Catholics, impede progress towards inter-communion and contravene Catholic principles of faith and order. Hopefully these essays may quieten some of this fear and ease the way for a more creative approach.

For Roman Catholics the significance of these issues is rather different. Few expect to see rapid changes in their own church structures but many sense a tension between on the one hand their own beliefs about God, ministry and women and on the other the assumptions that undergird the restriction of priesthood to men. The naming and working through of this conflict can be enormously exciting – as the essays by Janet Soskice, Alexina Murphy, Pia Buxton and Philip Holdsworth illustrate so well.

From the outset this book has been a deliberately ecumenical and inclusive venture with women and men, lay and ordained, Roman Catholic and Anglican working together. We hope others will now feel encouraged to join in.

Alyson Peberdy

The Ordination of Women and Anglican-Roman Catholic Dialogue

Christopher Hill

This chapter relates to the ordination of women in the context of the *official* dialogue between the Churches of the Anglican Communion and the Roman Catholic Church. I stress *official* – because that is what I know a little about and because we can all become the victims of personal theological opinions – whether for or against the ordination of women. In the Church of England we have suffered rather too much from protagonists or antagonists quoting their tame Roman Catholic theologians. And in any change of official relationship between our two Communions we have, in the end, to take the Churches as they officially are, as well as working for closer unity and convergence. I will also be confining myself to the world level, as this is for the foreseeable future the only level at which one can speak of an official Roman Catholic viewpoint on such an issue. I will begin by tracing the modest official discussion between the two Churches.

In July 1975 Archbishop Donald Coggan wrote to Pope Paul VI. The Archbishop informed the Pope of "the slow but steady growth of a consensus of opinion within the Anglican Communion that there are no fundamental objections in principle to the ordination of women to the priesthood". Four months later the Pope told the Archbishop that the Catholic Church "holds that it is not admissible to ordain women to the priesthood for very fundamental reasons''. The reasons included a male apostolate, the consistent practice of the Church, and the "living teaching authority which has consequently held that the exclusion of women from the priesthood is in accordance with God's plan for his Church''.

The correspondence was continued by the Archbishop of Canterbury in February 1976. Archbishop Coggan said, "We believe . . . unity will be manifested within a diversity of legitimate traditions because the Holy Spirit has never ceased to be active within the local Churches throughout the world. Sometimes what seems to one tradition to be a genuine expression of such a diversity in unity will appear to another tradition to go beyond the bounds of legitimacy.'' The Pope, in his reply, recognized the strong likelihood of ordination to the priesthood in some parts of the Communion. A realistic recognition as this indeed happened shortly afterwards in the USA and Canada. But Paul VI again spoke of "so grave a new obstacle and threat'' to reconciliation.

Between these two exchanges there had been what have come to be called "informal talks'' between staff of the Vatican Secretariat for Promoting Christian Unity and Anglicans responsible for the dialogue between the two Communions at the international level.

The meeting in November 1975 recommended that a small Joint Consultation should consider: "To what extent and in what ways churches with women priests and churches without women priests can be reconciled in sacramental fellowship.'' The so-called Versailles Consultation was to meet only at the end of February 1978, the idea of some consultation having been accepted by the Plenary Meeting of the Secretariat for Unity in Rome and the Standing Committee of the Anglican Consultative Council.

In the meantime the official Roman Catholic position had received clearer expression in the Declaration of the Sacred Congregation for the Doctrine of the Faith: *Inter Insigniores* of October 1976. Alongside the Declaration a commentary was also published. This, however, was unsigned and its status is far from clear: the commentary, nevertheless, does explicitly set the Declaration in the context of development within the Anglican Communion and cites the correspondence between Paul VI and Donald Coggan.

The Declaration itself is well known, but I would want to emphasize that a careful reading of *Inter Insigniores* reveals important lines of argument. The *first* reason given for rejecting women's ordination is the Church's constant tradition. I would only comment for the moment that the Declaration also acknowledges that the Magisterium had not felt the need to intervene until the present debate. The tradition is not, therefore, quite the same here as a tradition which includes the conscious decision of councils or popes. This is the first official statement on the subject it is unlikely to be the last. The *second* reason given is the attitude of Christ: that is to say an exclusively male apostolate. It is well known that the Pontifical Biblical Commission came to a slightly different conclusion and declared that the New Testament evidence was not itself decisive either for or against the ordination of women. The *third* reason is the teaching of the Apostles – especially Paul. The Declaration then looks at the permanent value of the attitude of Jesus and the Apostles. This is summarized and there is again a stress on Tradition: "it is a question of an unbroken tradition throughout the history of the Church, universal in the East and in the West". This norm is "considered to conform to God's plan for his Church". Here we have the identical words of Paul VI to Archbishop Coggan. It is interesting to speculate which were drafted first. It is only after all this that we have the rather complicated handling of ministerial priesthood, and sacramental and biblical symbolism. And all of *this* argument is only claimed to be illustrative: "it seems useful and opportune to *illustrate* this norm by showing the *profound fittingness* that theological reflection discovers. It is not a question here of bringing forward a demonstrative argument but of clarifying this teaching by the *analogy* of faith" (emphases mine). This is heavily coded but the message is clear. It is the unbroken tradition which is the prime argument. The Declaration does not claim the sacramental argument does more than show the appropriateness of maintaining the tradition.

I have already mentioned the origins of the Versailles Conversation. This was the first serious attempt to confront the question of the ordination of women at the level of the Anglican Communion and the world-wide Catholic Church. But it attempted this from the standpoint of a very specific question: could there be a sacramental relationship between Churches which did and did not ordain women to the priesthood. This may have been too restrictive but I believe that the work done at Versailles was not without value. I will quote the key paragraph as the document is not well known:

> Two things may be seen as ground for hope. First there is the fact that those Anglican churches which have proceeded to ordain women to the presbyterate have done so in the conviction that they have not departed from the traditional understanding of apostolic ministry (expressed for example in the Canterbury Statement of the Anglican-Roman Catholic International Commission). In the second place there is the fact that the recent Roman Catholic Declaration does not affirm explicitly that this matter is *de jure divino*. These facts would seem not to exclude the possibility of future developments.

I would underscore two things: Anglican provinces and individuals who have proceeded to the ordination of women have consistently stressed their action is a *development* of tradition, not a disjunction. The present Archbishop of Canterbury at the recent debate in the General Synod put it this way:

> We also owe it to the Roman Catholic and Orthodox Churches to take our decision on grounds of catholic order. If this decision is to be made it must not be made on the basis of a change in the character of priesthood but as an expansion of eligibility to the priesthood.

My *second* point is that the Versailles conversationalists did not lightly make the claim that *Inter Insigniores* did not go as far as to say that the exclusion of women from the priesthood was *de jure divino*. There were those on the Roman side who knew the precise history of the drafting of *Inter Insigniores* and they persuasively argued that this omission was significant. So grounds for hope were recognized.

Most unfortunately the final sentence of that crucial paragraph was ambiguous: mention of the ''possibility of future developments'' was not, I believe, intended to suggest that the Roman Catholic Church was about to change its practice. But the wording was read that way in Rome and so, later in the year, at the 1978 Lambeth Conference, the Official Roman Catholic delegation was obliged to soft-pedal the Report of the Versailles Consultation. An official statement was made to the Conference to the effect that the official position of the Roman Catholic Church on this matter ''was not destined to change''. But the ineligibility of women as not *de jure divino* was not disowned. This still seems to me to be of significance for the future. I shall return to this when I reach the work of ARCIC-II.

The following year, 1979, saw the publication of the Elucidations of ARCIC-I to the earlier Agreed Statements on Eucharist and Ministry. The Commission rightly or wrongly avoided a major discussion of the issue, but recognized that there had been rapid developments with regard to the ordination of women since the completion of its work on ministry in 1973. ARCIC *also* noted that those Anglican provinces which have ordained women to the presbyterate believe that their action implies no departure from the traditional doctrine of the ordained ministry. It contented itself with adding that the ordination of women did not affect its doctrinal agreement because the Commission was concerned with the origin and nature of ordained ministry not with who can or cannot be ordained. While ARCIC-I was right to stress that objections to the ordination of women are of a different kind from past Roman Catholic objections to the validity of Anglican

Orders, it is not difficult to see why some Anglican supporters of the ordination of women felt ARCIC had ducked the problem. Yet it is interesting that ARCIC-I cannot have seen the ordination of women as over-turning the nature of ministerial priesthood. Its silence was important.

When we look at the present Anglican-Roman Catholic International Commission it is clear that the ordination of women is a central issue. This was implicit in the mandate of ARCIC-II, the Common Declaration of Pope John Paul II and Archbishop Robert Runcie in Canterbury in 1982. They spoke of the agenda as including ''all that hinders the mutual recognition of the ministries of our Communions''. This necessarily involves the old question of *Apostolicae Curae* and the new question of the ordination of women.

The correspondence between Archbishop Runcie and both Pope John Paul II and Cardinal Willebrands now makes what was implicit explicit. In the exchange of letters with Cardinal Willebrands important issues are focused. The Archbishop notes his own cautions but speaks in the name of a Communion which includes provinces which do ordain women. He argues for the ordination of women on catholic grounds: namely, that the priest indeed represents Christ to the Church, especially in eucharistic presidency, but that it is the Risen and Ascended High Priesthood of Jesus which is thus represented. And at the Ascension Christ takes the *whole* of humanity with him into heaven, female as well as male. The basis of the argument is the patristic conviction that the incarnation is about the taking of the whole of humanity into the heavenly realms. The argument is not that an exclusively male priesthood cannot represent Christ's Ascended High Priesthood but that an inclusive priesthood would now do so more appropriately. The Cardinal of course agrees that one of the functions of the priesthood is to stand *in persona Christi* but argues that Christ's male identity is ''an inherent feature of the economy of salvation'' and that the sacramental ordination of men takes on force and significance because of ''the symbolic and iconic role of those who represent "Jesus Christ) in the eucharist". There is also argument from the responsive female imagery of the Church in Scripture. But once again it is interesting to see that the first reasons against the ordination of women given in the Cardinal's letter are related to Tradition: "The ordination only of men to presbyterate and episcopate is the unbroken Tradition of the Catholic and Orthodox Churches. Neither Church understands itself to be competent to alter this Tradition". The Cardinal goes on to add that the principal reason put forward in *Inter Insigniores* for resisting the ordination of women is indeed this tradition. I therefore see the symbolic and iconic arguments as essentially corroborative rather than demonstrative.

What does ARCIC-II do with all this? It has not yet definitely decided how to approach the ecumenical problem of the ordination of women. One way which has been proposed would be to look at what is required for communion. If indeed the ordination of women is contrary to catholic *faith* – I emphasize faith – there can be no communion or degrees of communion with a Church which either ordains women as a whole or in some of its provinces. But if it is not quite *de fide* that women cannot be ordained then there could – all other things being equal – be some degree of communion. Not I think full communion which would presuppose the full and mutual interchange ability of ministries, but some degree of communion between traditions which do and do not ordain women. This is no easy solution. It would raise very difficult questions for Anglicans favourable to the ordination of women – could they accept a degree of communion which would not give women priests recognition alongside men? But how could Rome recognize Anglican women priests while not allowing priestly vocation to her own daughters? One advantage of looking at the question from a *koinonia* framework is that it is realistic. I see no prospect of a change of practice in Rome in regard to the ordination of women in the foreseeable future. I *do*, however, see the theological question becoming more open. I have already spoken of a reticence to put the non-ordination of women at the level of faith.

Another important advantage of a *koinonia* framework is of a different order. The purpose of ecclesiastical communion is to be a sign to wider humanity of the communion God intends for the whole of creation. The Community of the whole of humanity is – amongst other things – a community of women and men. In this perspective women's ordination can be seen as something positive – a sign of God's Kingdom.

Others in ARCIC-II have expressed the view that the Commission should examine the question in itself and not be content with simply asking whether there can be any sacramental relationship between traditions which differ on this issue. Perhaps what we have here are not alternatives but short and long-term objectives for the dialogue between our Communions. In any case we need the humility to recognize that we are in the middle of a debate which may not be settled for some time. We need the humility to recognize that the ''reception'' of change and development in the Church is necessarily slow and cannot be wholly identified with magisteriums or synods. Rome will need to recognize that this issue will not fade away. So also Anglicans who are opposed. Those in favour, Catholics and Anglicans, will also need the humility to recognize the development may be wrong. If it is a false step, it will wither. Reception is very much the Gamaliel principle: if a thing is of men (or women) it will fail, but if it is of God it will not be overthrown.

I said a moment ago that I hoped the issue would gradually become more open theologically at the official level with the Roman Catholic Church. I don't think this is simply professional ecumenical optimism. The Roman Catholic Church already has a great experience of the ministry of women in the Church. Anglicans need to be rather humble about this. The contribution of women religious to mission, Catholic education and pastoral care is incalculable. The Roman Catholic Church also has a way of equipping the laity Anglicans need to pay regard to. It is not I believe without significance that women are now very extensively used as extraordinary ministers of the Eucharist throughout the Roman Catholic Church. This, incidentally, makes the row about female servers faintly ridiculous – if women can administer Holy Communion, they can do lesser tasks too. I note too that the new Roman Catholic code of Canon Law allows dispensation to *lay persons* to conduct weddings in the absence of a priest. The Code also allows lay persons to become diocesan chancellors. There are women chancellors in both our Churches in this country today. A chancellor shares a real jurisdiction with the bishop of the diocese. Its *potestas*. These are pointers to the fact that the debate and the experience are not static.

I must now begin to conclude. It is also time I slid a little off the fence – always a painful process. My *personal* conviction is that there are good theological reasons for advocating the ordination of women to the priesthood. I do not, therefore, think the ordination of women is plainly contrary to Catholic faith. But I do not believe in private judgement. My personal convictions must be submitted to the Church. Now while I recognize a deep loyalty to my mother church and to Anglicanism, in the end I believe in the One Holy Catholic and Apostolic Church, rather than any one province or denomination. So what the rest of the Church does is important for me.

While I do not unchurch those traditions which have a uniform ministry I recognize a special affinity on this issue with the Roman Catholic and Orthodox Churches because I believe we share the same ministry of bishops, priests and deacons. So the official rejection of the ordination of women by the Roman Catholic Church is more than simply an ecumenical problem because the verdict of the Roman Catholic Church is part of my evidence for deciding whether this is or is not a right development. While the Roman Catholic Church is officially against, I have hesitations about a too swift Anglican advance. I can only advance in a tentative manner with an open view of reception which might mean the wider acceptance of the ordination of women or the reverse. When I look at how the great decisions of history were made I accept the argument that ecumenical councils were not called before local change but to give or withhold Catholic endorsement to local development. I would plead for this *tentativeness* on the part of both protagonists and antagonists of women's ordination. Without such tentativeness we shall not easily discover whether the ordination of women is indeed in accordance with catholic faith or contrary to it.

Such a tentativeness will not be easy for those who believe strongly in their own or others' vocation. I recognize this. Nor will it be easy for those who have a deep conviction of the wrongness of the ordination of women.

Such tentativeness is appropriate because if I try to answer the question of whether the ordination of women is contrary to Catholic faith, the *official* Roman Catholic answer seems to be: we don't yet *know* with assurance whether it is in accordance or whether it is contrary to Catholic faith. The Roman Catholic Church is not about to change its *practice* because of the universal tradition: while theological reasons can be used to *illustrate* the appropriateness of maintaining the tradition of a male priesthood the theological reasoning does not seem to be the main reason for opposing this development. The diaconate for women does not appear to be a problem – and a major reason for this is the Byzantine tradition of a real women's diaconal ministry within the history of the Church. So we come at the end to questions of authority and the processes of change. Does the Church of God make changes only after completely conscious dogmatic reasoning. Or do changes intuitively happen which are then judged by the organs of the Church and the *sensus fidelium*?

And the final question is what and where is the Church. If, historically, change happens locally and is then judged universally, what counts as local experience? The Anglican Churches seem to be moving slowly towards the ordination of women – not without deep misgivings and hesitations on the part of some. Is *this* experience part of the evidence of the living Tradition of the Church – the community of the Holy Spirit. Does the experience of Churches not in communion with Rome count? Including the Churches of the Anglican Communion, which the Second Vatican Council declared to include essential Catholic ''structures''.

Nothing in Catholic theology or practice suggests the ossification of tradition – the view that because something has never happened before it can never ever happen. But the ministry and sacraments are essential for the cohesion of the Body of Christ. They should not be changed lightly. In the end we come down to how the instincts, experience, and theology of part of the Christian community are discerned by those who have authority in the Church and how both that experience and discernment are received by the whole Church. All this in a divided Christianity in which the organs of authority are necessarily impaired by schism – neither Anglicans nor Roman Catholics would claim that either Roman magisterium or synodical government are perfect models and examples of authority. So you will see why my priorities are still ecumenical, because in the end I think the problem is one of tradition, authority and where you find the Church. Because my imperative remains the search for the wholeness of Christian unity, those who are committed to the ordination of women will have to try to understand my ''reticence''. For me ''Catholic faith'' cannot be known with assurance outside the unity of the *whole* Church. I recognize the experience of those Anglican Churches which ordain women. But while Christian opinion remains divided, I cannot yet say the ordination of women is in accordance with Catholic faith – but nor am I saying it is against. We are still in the middle of a long process of discernment. All of us, whether for or against, have to live with this tension until the mind of the whole Church is clear.

This chapter was first presented as a paper to the Anglican-Roman Catholic conference held at Heythrop College in March 1987.

2

Would the Symbolism Be All Wrong?

Janet Martin Soskice

Many non-Roman Catholics assume that all Roman Catholics are opposed to the ordination of women. Many Roman Catholics are surprised by this assumption. Certainly the official pronouncements one sees cited in the press seem uniform in their opposition but, as befits a "Catholic" church, there is much reflection and questioning amongst laity, priests, religious and theologians that goes quietly on in the background. The quietness of the discussion may have led some to conclude there is no discussion at all. The Roman Catholic situation contrasts with that in the Church of England – in the latter other features of church life and organization have pushed the question of women's ordination into high relief, the debate has become partisan – one must be either pro or contra. Roman Catholic discussions in this country have been, in my experience, more subdued: the same person can in discussion still say, "On the one hand . . . then, on the other." Similarly the Roman Catholic discussion has been spared the misleading polarization, particularly favoured in some quarters of the press, which puts theological liberals on one side of the discussion and theological conservatives on the other, so that everyone who is for the ordination of women is presented as doubting the virgin birth, the incarnation, the resurrection, and so on, and everyone who opposes women's ordination believing all these things. This polarization is a completely inaccurate representation even of the Anglican debate. There is no direct correlation between favouring women's ordination and doubting resurrection faith. Roman Catholics for their part have had to take account of an increasingly vocal group of nuns whose piety and orthodoxy cannot be discounted, yet who wish for women's ordination.

I am not, in presenting the Roman Catholic discussion as more subdued, claiming any greater merit for it; it may be in part cowardice, it is probably more to do with the fact that any real prospect of the ordination of women looks remote indeed and the matter is in that sense "academic". The point I wish to make is that it simply hasn't been as hot a topic there as in Anglican circles.

But it is a genuine topic, and one that attracts increasing interest in all sectors of the Church's life. Paradoxically, since the publication in 1976 of the document, *Inter Insigniores: Declaration on the Admission of Women to the Ministerial Priesthood*, which might have been thought to put a damper on things, there's been more interest in the subject not less. This is at least partly because that document made it clear that the issue was more than just women, but concerned the whole nature of the ministerial priesthood. Indeed for the theologians the question "is the ordination of women contrary to Catholic faith", is not one question but many, towards which Biblical scholars, ecclesiologists, ancient historians and liturgists are all in their various ways contributing.

I wish to address just one piece of the puzzle, and indeed will be able to consider even that one piece only partially, and it is the question of whether the symbolism would be all wrong if one had women priests. Before doing so, however, I should like to address two preliminaries.

The first is to ask why consideration of the ordination of women is so involved? Surely the Catholic theologian need only look at Scripture and tradition, at what has always been held by the Church? However, the theologian's task is rarely so straightforward. It's not just a question of what has always been held but also of whether that is essential to the faith, and this is not always readily determined. For example, the consensus of Scripture and centuries of Catholic teaching once was that slavery was not contrary to Catholic faith. With a little historical imagination one can see why; scripture seems to condone it, Christ nowhere tries to overthrow it, Christians everywhere accepted it as an unavoidable, if not necessarily desirable, feature of life. As late as 1866 the Holy Office stated that slavery was "not at all contrary to the natural and divine law", then in 1891 slavery was condemned and is now regarded as contrary to Catholic faith.[1] Looking at what scripture seemed to teach and what the Church consistently held concerning slavery did not of itself provide the final resolution to this problem, although of course it informed it.

One could say, however, that attitudes towards slavery are a different matter from attitudes towards the ordination of women, that the former is not as central to the church's faith. This is on the face of it a somewhat alarming claim; that the enslavement of others should matter less to us than who should be allowed to preside and preach, but it is perhaps reasonable to say that slavery is not *doctrinally* of the same consequence as women's ordination.

Let us then take another example, that of the Church's response to Darwinism and evolutionary theory. It is hard now for us to imagine how big a shock and a heresy these ideas seemed to all kinds of Christians. Our forebears in the faith would have for the most part found it inconceivable that someone could doubt the physical descent of all humanity from the one man, Adam, and the one woman, Eve, and still call themselves Catholic Christians. Scripture and tradition appeared united in their teaching about the origins of the physical world and man's place within it; this teaching was challenged *fundamentally* by evolutionary theory. If one was to be reconciled in any way to these new scientific ideas, enormous theological readjustment was called for, and not simply in discovering non-literal readings for the first chapters of Genesis. Even more threatening was the challenge to doctrine. What account, theologians had to ask, can you give of original sin and of our culpability if you no longer take the Adam and Eve story as historically true? How can you argue that man is uniquely in the image of God if he crawled out of the evolutionary sludge with the other beasts? Theologians are still working on the theological questions involved in a rapprochement with evolutionary theory; issues to do with theology of creation, doctrine of man, free will and determinism, responsibility for sin – issues far more central to Christian faith than those surrounding the ordination of women. The theological task in coming to terms with modern scientific views has not been to abandon scripture and tradition, but to re-understand what we take to be essential to them. I suggest that the same process is going on now as we try to re-understand the issues surrounding the ordination of women.

The second preliminary concerns the difficult word "equality". Sometimes one gets the impression that the main argument for the ordination of women is a very crude argument about equal rights – namely, just as women should be allowed to be executives for TWA and to be fork-lift truck drivers, they should be ordained. I personally have never heard an *advocate* of women's ministry use this crude argument, although I've heard many opponents of women's ordination cite it. The kinds of things I characteristically hear from the women (and men) whom I teach seem to be that they want to be involved in the central Christian task of bringing Christ to people in word and sacrament. They say, "We have been taught to see Christ in all people – the suffering, the dying, the slum-dwellers of Calcutta – why not in women?" They do not characteristically say that women should be ordained because women are just the same as men, but rather because they're different, with different gifts and insights to body forth Christ in the Church and the world. They say that all of us would be enriched if women could break the bread with us and preach the word to us, and that all of us are the poorer that they do not. If these are arguments about equality then they certainly are not the brassy, careerist "me-tooism" that they are sometimes made out to be. Indeed, it would be odd if people who held the priestly office in such esteem should have crudely careerist ideas about it – as though the same people who argue for the ordination of women might well petition the Royal Shakespeare Company to cast a woman as Hamlet!

Perhaps it is better to speak of *dignity*. What women do want is to see their lives as fully and equally places where Christ is present to the world. They want to be assured that the Church respects their full human dignity, their equality in that sense. I might add that I have never met an opponent of women's priestly ministry whose main argument was that women were *inferior* or unequal to men, who didn't want to accord full dignity to women and women's lives. The Vatican document, *Inter Insigniores* is explicit in asserting this, as is subsequent papal teaching. The argument of the opponent is rather that each sex is equal but different, and (this is important) different in a way decisive to the suitability for priestly ministry.

Here is where the argument from symbolism enters in, and to it we now turn. *Inter Insigniores* says this:

> The priest, in the exercise of his ministry . . . represents Christ, who acts through him. . . . It is this ability to represent Christ that St. Paul considered as characteristic of his apostolic function.

The supreme expression of this is the Eucharist where the priest takes the role of Christ "to the point of being his very image, when he pronounces the words of consecration. . . . The Christian priesthood is therefore of a sacramental nature: the priest is a sign, the supernatural effectiveness of which comes from the ordination received, but a sign that must be perceptible and which the faithful must be able to recognize with ease". If the role of Christ were not taken by a man, "it would be difficult to see in the minister the image of Christ. For Christ himself was and remains a man".[2]

The document goes on to point out that Jesus did not

himself choose any female apostles and suggests that this was not for any sociological reasons to do with the acceptability of women in his own place and culture, but because women could not be his image in the requisite way.

Several immediate rebuttals occurred to many who read *Inter Insigniores*. We might summarize some of them thus: "Jesus was also young, Jewish, as far as we know physically fit. He didn't choose any disciples who were gentile, elderly or lame. We have been taught to see Christ in everyone. We speak readily of seeing Christ in the saints, both male and female. Why is it then that an elderly, stout, Chinese man can image Christ to me in a way that Mother Teresa of Calcutta cannot?"

To give the document its due we should note that it suggests that sacramental signs are more than just conventional. This is what one would expect, for if it were only a matter of perceptions then perceptions shift. "There was an early controversy in the Eastern Church over whether all priests must be bearded since Christ was bearded, and the priest must be the image of Christ to the people. But sacramental signs are not just *perceptual* signs (in the sense that might rule out perceptually Chinese, stout, beardless, or elderly), they are deeper, one might say *ontological* signs. There must be an essential appropriateness to sacramental signs and it is suggested that it is essentially inappropriate for a woman to be the image of Christ. (I use the term "essential" in its more philosophical sense, "being of the essence".)

Here church tradition can be brought in, for it has been the opinion of theologians throughout the ages that women would be unsuitable as symbols for Christ. Now it would be misleading to suggest that theologians throughout the ages have ceaselessly discussed the possibility of the ordination of women and rejected it, rather, as *Inter Insigniores* points out, "we are dealing with a debate which classical theology scarcely touched upon" (*I.I.*, 332). It almost never occurred to anyone before recent times to ask whether women could be priests. Indeed "women" in general or "the place of women in the Church" was not a topic for the classical theologians as was, for instance, Christology or Trinity or the nature of grace. The remarks we have from the theological tradition on women are, therefore, somewhat incidental, but nonetheless highly illuminating.

For example, it is something of a shock to discover that a number of the Fathers did not believe that women were fully in the image of God. Their opinion was in part based on texts like I Corinthians 11:7: "For man ought not to cover his head, since he is the image and glory of God, but woman is the glory of man."

This text in itself would seem insufficient evidence to adduce that women were not fully in the image of God, but we must consider its being read in a world where the natural inferiority of women was taken as a matter of fact. Aristotle, who argued about most things, didn't even feel a need to argue about it. In the Mediterranean world of Jesus's time women were not only held to be physically and emotionally weaker than men, but to lack the full complement of reason.[3]

Theologians from Augustine to Aquinas would have agreed with Aristotle that women are inferior in rationality and subordinate by nature in the scheme of things. There seemed strong scriptural warrant for these conclusions, which the theologians cited; it was, after all, Adam who was made first and he named the animals, indicating his authority over all creatures. It was the weaker sex whom Satan tempted and who first fell. It was through the frailty of the woman, Eve, that death entered the world. After the Fall, woman's subordination to the man was heightened by the longing she would feel towards him and the pain she would suffer in childbirth (Gen. 3:16). The Fathers for the most part preferred the creation narrative of Genesis 2, where Eve is created second and from Adam's rib, to that of Genesis 1 where it is said, "So God created man in his own image, in the image of God he created him; male and female he created them" (Gen. 1:27).

Women were regarded by many early theologians as subordinate in the order of creation and as lesser in authority, rationality and will. God, on the other hand, was known as supremely powerful, supremely good, and supremely rational. It is no wonder that these theologians doubted if women were fully in the image of God. This may explain a medieval ruling in church law that says that a woman may not make religious vows without a man's permission: "It is the natural order among humans that women be subject to their husbands and children to their parents, because it is only right in such matters that the greater serve the lesser . . . woman was not made in God's image."[4]

The natural subordination of women should not be misunderstood as a prejudice of a few benighted theologians, it was a standard feature of an earlier world view, secular and religious – Chrysostom, Augustine, and Aquinas all held that women were naturally subordinate to men. And it is important to note that this subordination was not judged to be that of equal to equal, but of natural inferior to natural superior. Aquinas ties exclusion of women from the priesthood to this explicitly: "It is not possible for the female sex to signify eminence of degree as it is characterised by the state of submission."[5] For Aquinas the symbolism would be all wrong. Women cannot signify Christ because they are naturally subordinate. They are of low degree. This, if anything, has been the constant position of the Church and the main argument why the symbolism would be wrong.

If it shocks us that anyone or any class should be thought unsuitable for priestly ministry because of their low status we can also ponder Pope Leo the Great's angry remarks about slaves "raised to the dignity of the priesthood, as if servile vileness could lawfully receive this honour. . . . There is a double wrong in this matter, that the sacred ministry is polluted by such vile company, and the rights of owners are violated."[6] The point of such citations is not to demonstrate how miserably sexist or elitist the Church has been. That would be anachronistic for these theologians were men of their own times. Rather it is to suggest that

what are appropriate symbols in the sixth century or the
twelfth may be inappropriate now, if based on assumptions
now widely thought to be contrary to Catholic faith.

To conclude, if women are judged to be inappropriate as
symbols for Christ in the Eucharist the difference from men
on which such a judgement rests can't be incidental (like
being Chinese, Jewish, or old), but must be fundamental.
Church tradition suggests that the essential and natural
subordination of women makes them inappropriate as
images for God and Christ. The Roman Catholic Church
has never consistently taught, until late in this century, that
women were equal to men, but just different. In this the
Church has been no worse than any secular institution; the
law, the universities, the government.[7] The question for us
now and a question that is preliminary to that of the
ordination of women, is, do we any longer believe that
women are essentially inferior to men? The Holy Office does
not. But if we now want to say, as they do, that men and
women are equal but different, have different ministries but
with equality of honour, what we cannot honestly claim is
that this is the tradition of the Church. The tradition, if any,
has been that women were unsuitable for priesthood being
essentially subordinate. Arguments for excluding women
from priestly ministry premised on the ''different but equal''
basis are no less modern, no more traditional, than
arguments for the ordination of women.[8]

Indeed we might now wish to argue that as far as
symbolism goes, the priest represents Christ not by virtue of
his eminence but by virtue of his humility, and from this
conclude that those who the world holds in least esteem – the
poor, the enslaved and (in many parts of today's world)
women, are the ideal candidates for symbolizing Christ to
us. This is just one of the many arguments for the ordination
of women that arise from a consideration of symbolism. I
cannot go into all these now. My point has been, more
modestly, to suggest that the debate is still at best *wide open*
on this subject of symbolism. One could go further and say
that the debate is a bleeding wound as Catholics are forced

to look at features of our tradition in which we can now take little pride.

NOTES

1. See John Wijngaards, *Did Christ Rule Out Women Priests?*, rev. edn. (Great Wakering: McCrimmon Publishing Co. Ltd, 1986) pp. 49–51.
2. *Inter Insigniores*, in *Vatican Council II: More Post Conciliar Documents*, ed. Austin Flannery, O.P. (Leominster: Fowler Wright Books Ltd, 1982) p. 339.
3. See W.W. Fortenbaugh, ''Aristotle on Slaves a1 d Women'', in *Articles on Aristotle*, Vol. II, ed. J. Barnes, M. Schofield, R. Sorabji (London: Gerald Duckworth & Co. Ltd, 1979).
4. Gratian's Decree, cited by Margaret Brennan, ''Enclosure: Institutionalising the Invisibility of Women in Ecclesiastical Communities'', in *Women: Invisible in Church and Theology*, Concilium, December, 1985, ed. E. Schussler Fiorenza and M. Collins (Edinburgh: T. and T. Clark Ltd, 1985) p. 41.
5. Cited by Wijngaards, *op. cit.*, p. 61.
6. Cited by G.E.M. de Ste. Croix, *The Class Struggle in the Ancient Greek World* (London: Gerald Duckworth & Co. Ltd, 1981; second impression, 1983) p. 422.
7. Memories are short in politics as elsewhere, but many will still recall the horror some felt at the suggestion that women be admitted to the House of Lords as peeresses in their own right.
8. The ''separate spheres'' argument often employed in this context has its own difficulties, see Janet Radcliffe Richards, ''Separate Spheres'', in Peter Singer, ed., *Applied Ethics* (Oxford University Press, 1986).

3

Priesthood and the Gospel Ministry of Word and Sacrament

Philip Holdsworth

The question of ordaining women to the priesthood has come to the fore in recent years. After nearly forty years in the Roman Catholic priesthood I believe I can write from some experience of its exercise. What I want to do is to look at the place of priests in the Catholic system, to note what priesthoods there were in the New Testament and to note also that the Gospel ministry of word and sacrament was not originally called a priesthood. There will emerge that, in my view, there is no objection in principle in Catholic doctrine to the ordination of women to the presbyterate.

The idea of priesthood and its practice are found very widely among religions. They are commonly connected with sacrifices. Sometimes it is the father of a family or the head of a tribe that performs the priestly functions but often there is a separate order or caste established to see to these. As with ancient classical pagan religions so with that of Israel. Patriarchal priesthood is recorded as the first form it took, but the Levitical priesthood was eventually formed on well-organized lines, the Levites (tribe of Levi) taking charge of the services of the Tabernacle and only the descendants of Aaron, real or supposed, exercising the priestly, sacrificial roles. With the development of the importance of the Sanctuary and especially of the Temple, the importance of the priests also grew and in particular that of the High Priest who alone could enter the Holy of Holies on the day of Atonement.

This system of priesthood is well known to us in the New Testament because of the accounts of the hostility encountered from it by Jesus. It is treated as the official element of Judaism and sometimes regarded as at least rendered superfluous by the definitive action of Jesus in his death and resurrection.

What other priesthoods are known to the New Testament? There are two which certainly should have our attention. The first of these is the priesthood of Jesus as it is presented in the Epistle to the Hebrews. Let us look at this carefully. Jesus is declared to be "the apostle and high priest of our religion", "the supreme high priest who has gone through the highest heavens", "one tempted in every way that we are, though he is without sin". But there is all the difference between his priesthood and the Levitical. Moses was faithful as a servant, but Christ as a son, and is that much the greater. He was indeed given priesthood as was Aaron, but his was of a higher order. He was given the "title of high priest of the order of Melchisedech" and the point about this is that Melchisedech "has no father, mother or ancestry, and his life has no beginning or ending; he is like the Son of God. He remains a priest for ever". Moreover, Jesus came from the tribe of Judah and not of Levi, so was not eligible for the Levitical priesthood – in Judaism he was a layman only. But now he has a priesthood that he cannot lose: "The Lord has sworn an oath which he will not retract, thou art a priest for ever according to the order of Melchisedech", "raised above the heavens, one who would not need to offer sacrifices every day, as the other high priests do for their own sins and then for those of the people, because he has done this once and for all by offering himself". This is guaranteed by the oath the Lord has sworn.

The priesthood of Jesus puts him outside any organized cultic priesthood, it is a transcendental priesthood. The Epistle to the Hebrews sums it up: "All the priests stand at their duties every day, offering over and over again the same sacrifices which are quite incapable of taking sins away. He on the other hand has offered one single sacrifice for sins and then taken his place for ever 'at the right hand of God'.''

We do well to reflect frequently on Jesus, the one eternal High Priest, once for all taking sins away: ''By virtue of that one single offering he has achieved the eternal perfection of all whom he is sanctifying.'' This is the first priesthood of the New Testament and the paramount one at that. What other priesthood does it have? The second occurs in several parts of the New Testament. It is mentioned in I Peter 2 ''a royal priesthood'', Apoc. 1:6 ''he has made us a line of kings, priests to serve his God''. These texts recall Exodus 19:6 ''I will count you a kingdom of priests, a consecrated nation''. The Decree on Priests of Vatican II expounds the matter (No. 2) ''The Lord Jesus whom the Father has made holy and sent into the world (Jn X 36) has made his whole mystical body share in the anointing of the Spirit with which he himself has been anointed. For in him all the faithful are made a holy and royal priesthood. They offer spiritual sacrifices to God through Jesus Christ and they proclaim the perfections of him who has called them out of darkness into his marvellous light.''

The essential priesthood of the New Covenant is that of Jesus who is uniquely priest by right and by nature. Then comes the derived priestly character of the whole people of God, all who are incorporated in Christ and for that reason participate as a body in his priesthood.

If this is so whence come all the priests attested by later history? The Roman Catholic and Orthodox Churches have them in plenty, even now. The Anglicans often, but not invariably, refer to their ministers as ''priests''. How has all this come about?

We know very little about arrangements made personally by Jesus for the ensuing gospel ministry. He chose a dozen apostles, gave them power to preach and cast out evil spirits. Peter was given a certain prominence. Later Jesus commanded them to repeat his last supper, also to make disciples of all nations, to baptize them and teach them his commandments. He promised to be ''with them'' as long as would be necessary.

As time went on we find the disciples adding to the number of apostles and also setting up a supplementary group, the deacons. We don't know much about the structure of ministerial arrangements in the early decades but we come across πρεσβυτεροι, "presbyters", who led and guided the communities, exercising some authority. Sometimes we meet also ἐπισκοποι, "overseers", who may perhaps be identified with the presbyters or with the more prominent ones. By the second century the three-fold order of ἐπισκοποι, πρεσβυτεροι, and διακονοι, bishops, elders and deacons was coming into existence. But the word "priest" seems not to have been used until the end of the century and at first it was used only of bishops, the presbyters being thought of as delegated adjuncts of the bishop. It was the spread of Christianity from the cities to the countryside and the consequent founding of churches away from the episcopal church that threw into relief the figure of the parish presbyter, operating in greater separation from the bishop, although authorized by him. As we know, this development had a great future before it and is indeed still with us. The use of the term *sacerdos* (ιερευς), a word referring to a cultic priesthood, began as an allegorical expression applied to the bishop[1] and later was used for presbyters operating by themselves. St Augustine seems to have had hesitation about the use of the term[2] at least if it is thought to imply that bishops or presbyters mediate between Christ and the community.

Should we deprecate the use of the term "priest" (derived incidentally from "presbyter") to designate the Christian minister of word and sacrament? Was it a legitimate development? It depends how we understand the term. In so far as a ministerial priest has and exercises the powers that derive (through the bishops and initially the apostles) from Christ, the eternal and unique priest, powers conferred for the benefit of the Christian community and its mission to the world, then he may be termed a priest in that strictly limited and secondary sense. But there are dangers in this usage. It can encourage inattention to and

neglect of the radical and universal priesthood of Jesus and
to the derived, but also universal, priesthood of the people
of God. In fact the presbyteral ministry exists to promote
knowledge of these and fuller participation in them. I am
accepting that there is need for a ministerial role for certain
believers, designated by the church communities, though
receiving their authority and powers from God through
Jesus Christ, and these authorizations and powers concern
principally the commission to preach the gospel *ex officio*; to
absolve from sins; to lead the eucharistic celebration and to
anoint the gravely ill. All of these go very closely together
and are the way Jesus, the one full priest, is made present
to his people and activates its priesthood.

Now it is time to turn to the question of the place of
women in the ministry. It is clear that women were closely
involved in the mission of Jesus: his mother and Elizabeth,
the Samaritan woman, the Mary who sat at his feet
listening, the one who anointed him with oil, the one who
washed his feet with her tears, Mary Magdalen at the
tomb, the other women at the Cross and at the tomb. The
evangelists don't offer them as major figures in the story
but they could not omit them. But what of the early years
of the Church? Do we hear of them as ministers? Very
little, and there are passages in St Paul's writings which
suggest a ban on women exercising the ministry. St Paul is
commonly thought of as having been the chief and
unequivocal opponent of women's ministry but recently
this has been questioned and a new study of the texts has
been undertaken. And to be fair to St Paul, one may recall
the many names of women helpers in the work of
evangelization that he acknowledges in his epistles, the
titles of ''deacon'' and ''apostle'' being used for them
sometimes. Although there are indications that they were
more acceptable in the Johannine community there is not a
great deal of evidence for women in the early ministry. In
later centuries we do come across phenomena like the
exercise of jurisdiction by abbessess and the making of
consecrated Cathusian nuns into deacons or deaconesses,

who were allowed to read the Gospel at matins (though not at mass) wearing a stole, which is usually seen as a sacerdotal vestment. But all this is marginal and seems to reflect social or monastic rather than theological concerns. The real breakthrough comes with the decisions in this century of the churches of the Reformation, including some Anglican provinces, to opt for the availability of presbyteral ordination for women, "Women Priests", as we commonly call them.

What of the Roman Catholic Church? Here there is far less widespread movement but it exists among a number, and has backing by reputable theologians, although some Roman Catholic feminists take the view that the arrival of women in the ministry must await the dismantling of objectionable and unessential features of the hierarchical structures which, however ancient, have no permanent validity in a truly catholic system. I would quote items 12 and 13 of the specific proposals that emanated from the Laity Consultation held in Oxford in 1986.

12)   The Church's avowed concern for justice and peace in the world should be shown in its own structures, particularly in its attitude to women and minorities, who are excluded and alienated from the mainstream of Church life.
13)   In the present situation of grave shortage of priests there should be a re-appraisal of the eligibility of married men and women for ordination to the priesthood and the diaconate.[3]

So much for a particular group of Catholics, speaking on their own authority but after reflection and discussion. What of the official Church? Let us consider a paragraph from section 6 of the recent Roman Synod's treatment of the "Church as Communion".

There has often been question in these last years of the vocation and mission of women in the Church. The

Church should see that women take their place in the
Church in such a way that they can adequately use their
proper gifts for the service of the Church and have a more
extensive part in the various fields of the Church's
apostolate. Pastors should gratefully take up and
encourage the collaboration of women in the work of the
Church.

This may sound both patronising and hesitant but it does, as
it stands, open the way for the possibility of women's
presbyteral ordination. Of course it depends how one
interprets the expression "use their proper gifts for the
service of the Church". Some would insist it refers only to
those roles that have hitherto been recognized as open to
women. However, as it stands, the statement does not
exclude the exploration of other ways in which women could
contribute to the life of the Church and indeed might seem to
suggest it. Nowadays the debate has got under way and the
arguments are freely bandied to and fro. Recently a group of
theologians in this country, including two Jesuit scholars,
declared their support for the Church of England's efforts to
resolve the questions raised and in particular commended
the statement of the Dean of King's College, London, Revd.
Richard Harries, in answer to the Bishop of London's
opposition to the move to ordain women. (See Appendix.)
   I think that there are two especial points that need to be
cleared up. One is the objection that to ordain women now is
to go against nearly 2,000 years of tradition. Tradition is
often appealed to here. But tradition is the constant teaching
of the Church as manifested against the mistaken
divagations from it, the heresies. There was no general
attempt until recently to propose the ordination of women. It
was the *practice* of the Church never to do this but there was
no general teaching about it, as it was never challenged,
practice, then, rather than formal tradition.
   Another point made is that the priest functions *in persona
Christi* and that to do this with full symbolism the priest must
be a man not a woman. This seems to give too much

importance to sexual differentiation. The ministry needs a human being not a monkey and men and women are both fully human.

From a talk given to the Newman Society, Oxford, 9 February 1986.

NOTES

1. See E. Schillebeeckx, *The Church with a Human Face* (London: SCM 1985) p. 145.
2. Ibid., p. 144.
3. See *The Tablet*, 1 February 1986, p. 114.
4. See *The Tablet*, 8 February 1986, p. 140.

Women, the Bible and the Priesthood

John and Gillian Muddiman

Introduction

From among the many issues raised by the current debate on the priesthood of women, two specifically biblical themes form the subject of this study, the notions of priestly holiness and spiritual authority. These themes, as we shall show, have firm roots in the biblical material, but also undergo major changes and developments. We are convinced that they lie behind several of the so called "theological objections" to the ordination of women; and, even more importantly perhaps, that they contribute to the almost instinctive feeling, on the part of many who hold a catholic view of the Ministry, that women are less appropriate than men as vehicles of that ritual purity and spiritual power which priestly ordination symbolizes and conveys. It is the aim of this study to show that, far from debarring women from the Christian priesthood, a proper appreciation of the biblical tradition in the relevant areas weighs in favour of their admission.

Before turning to our themes, it may be helpful to offer some introductory comments on the peculiar problem posed by the use of biblical and theological arguments in this debate. Their characteristic effect has been to absolutize opposing positions and render them atemporal, rigid, and immune to practical considerations. On the one hand, opponents of the priesthood of women have convinced themselves that they are justified in making a stand of conscience against majority opinion in their communions because fundamental principles of Christian doctrine are at stake.[1] Ordinations of women, they imply, not only invalidate ministry in the churches which permit them, but even constitute an act of apostasy. On the other hand, proponents of women's ordination can occasionally use theological arguments in such a way as to imply that until women are ordained and wholeness of representation restored to the ministry, it remains fundamentally defective, just as, on this showing, it has been since the inception of the Christian Church. The underlying assumption of both positions is the same, that biblical revelation and theological reflection somehow occur in a timeless vacuum. What this essay sets out to illustrate is the need for a more developmental hermeneutic – one which takes fully into account the time factor in interpretation. We emphasize, for instance, the temporally conditioned nature of Israel's thinking about perfection in those species, human and animal, which are sexually differentiated; and the temporally conditioned character of the early Church's initial reluctance to use the language of priesthood to describe ministerial office. But our response is neither to consign the biblical material to the dustbin of history, nor to attempt to turn the clock back to a supposed golden age in the past, but to listen as attentively as we can to what is really being said in Scripture about priestly holiness and spiritual authority, and to ask how in our changed and changing circumstances these insights are to be re-appropriated and applied.

The Old Testament and Priestly Holiness

The understanding of ministerial priesthood, as it has developed in Christianity, owes much to the Old Testament. By stressing this at the outset, we are not thereby seeking to discredit the development. On the contrary, catholic Christianity, as opposed to *Marcionism* in its ancient or modern forms, has rightly built on Old as well as New Testament foundations. When the framework of Jewish institutions was dissolved in the early Church, above all when the Jerusalem Temple was destroyed, it was historically inevitable and religiously proper for Christian replacements to be found. If the holiness and beauty of worship and the symbolic interlocking of the spiritual and the material was to be preserved, a Christian equivalent of the Levitical priesthood had to emerge. Certain aspects of the tradition, most obviously blood sacrifice, were immediately recognized as non-transferable to the new situation. Others were allowed to continue because the issue of their legitimacy was of no practical consequence in the prevailing conditions of the time. One such, we claim, was the exclusion of women from the priesthood.

It is an undeniable fact that the Old Testament did not allow women to be priests. The exclusion of women is taken for granted to such a degree that it is nowhere specifically prescribed. It is assumed that priests are drawn from the congregation of the Israelite people, of which only adult males were full members. It was not the case that women were excluded from all participation in the cult; they had their own specific functions at certain festivals, and could in rare circumstances take on a more usually male role such as that of cult prophet. There are, however, no circumstances envisaged in the Old Testament when a woman could conceivably fulfil a priestly function. We, therefore, need to ask the question: is the prohibition of women priests in the Old Testament essential and intrinsic to the faith and practice of Israel's religion as it was carried over into Christianity? Or, is it, like so much of the cultic law of the Old Testament, part of a culturally conditioned network of regulations which have been superseded under the New Covenant?

Let us first note that it was not only women who were barred from the priesthood. Leviticus 21 gives us the rules governing the selection and conduct of priests. In order to be a priest, a man has to fulfil certain conditions. He must be descended from Aaron. He may only marry a virgin, not a widow or divorcee. He may not defile himself by contact with a dead body, except that of a close relative, and even this is forbidden to the High Priest. Most significantly, a man who has any physical deformity or skin blemish may not be a priest. The examples of disqualifying deformities given include an injured foot or hand, defective eyesight, crushed testicles, and itching diseases. This then is the crucial qualification for being a priest according to the Old Testament; the priest must be without blemish: not just a man, but a perfect specimen of manhood.

If we read on in Leviticus to the next chapter, we discover an interesting connection. The regulations governing the choice of an animal for sacrifice correspond very closely to those for qualification for the priesthood. Like the priest, the animal to be sacrificed must be without blemish. Again, disabilities specified are blindness, itching, crushed testicles and so on. So we find that just as the priest must be a perfect specimen of manhood, so the animal must be a perfect unblemished example of its kind. The reason for the injunctions in both cases is explained by the opening command of God: "You shall be holy to me; for I the LORD am holy." The idea seems to be that there is an intrinsic connection between God and his people, the two parties to the Covenant. As God is holy, so the people must be holy. Ideally, Israel is a "holy nation". However, the reality is necessarily imperfect. So the priesthood represents the people in their covenant relationship with God, symbolizing the theoretical sanctity of the whole people. The main function of the priesthood was, by sacrifice and worship, continually to re-establish the holiness of the people. Similarly, the offering to be presented to God must also be pure and holy. The basic ideas behind the concept of holiness in the Old Testament are those of separateness, wholeness, completion. This is exemplified by the confusing dietary and other laws, where there are prohibitions which seem at first sight totally pointless, e.g. the prohibition in Lev. 19:19 against growing two kinds of seed in one field, and some of the regulations concerning clean and unclean animals. The reasoning behind all this becomes clear when it is seen that it is mixing and confusion of the created order which is condemned. The unclean animals are ones which are imperfect members of their class, or which do not fit with the general scheme of classification. The categories of creation must be kept distinct; only those men and animals which are perfect examples of their class may approach God or be offered to him.[2]

This seems to have led us a long way from the issue of women priests, but in fact the same basic motivation lies behind the barring of women from the priesthood. The Old Testament writers feel that women are not perfect specimens of humankind, but are secondary to men in creation. Woman is by her very nature imperfect. Any bodily emission, particularly involving blood, is regarded as defiling. We noted earlier that a man with an injured, i.e. bleeding foot or hand, could not fulfil a priestly function. Women are hence ritually unclean for a good proportion of their adult life and are, therefore, disqualified from the priesthood not on the grounds of their sex alone, but on the basis of the same rules which govern the selection of men as priests. It seems to us that this is a clear example of the kind of culturally conditioned regulation which is not binding for the modern Church. We no longer examine male candidates for the priesthood for spots and pimples or disqualify them if they are short-sighted. Much of the motivation behind the barring of women is of that order, connected with primitive ideas of holiness and purity which are no longer relevant. A woman's menstruation no longer seems the mysterious, uncontrollable, defiling occurrence that it was to the Israelites. We know exactly what causes it, how it works, and how to control it.

We mentioned earlier that another idea behind the concept of holiness was that of separateness. God says to Israel, "I am the LORD your God, who have separated you from the peoples. You shall therefore make a distinction between the clean beast and the unclean . . ." (Lev.

20:24 – 5). This idea of Israel as a separated nation distinct from others around it is vital for understanding the Old Testament, and provides us with a second motivation for the exclusion of women from the priesthood. The nation of Israel began its life as a religious group fighting to establish for itself a national identity in a hostile environment. Consequently Old Testament religion defines itself in opposition to the religion of surrounding peoples, notably the Canaanites, and distinguishes itself in many cases sharply from Canaanite cultic practices. Anything, therefore, which could possibly be connected with the Mother-Goddess, fertility-cult type of religion exemplified by the Canaanites was anathema to Israel. What better way to distinguish one's worship from that of a fertility religion than to deny a place to women in the most central and holy part of the cult? Women's connection with fertility cults is very common. Menstruation was seen as related to the cyclic rhythm of the cosmos and phases of the moon. Blood too had an intrinsic link with fertility. In some rituals blood could be poured on the ground to make it fertile, and indeed we find even in the Old Testament the idea that the life and vitality of any human being or animal consists in the blood.

Again, we seem to be dealing with a historically and culturally conditioned taboo – an exclusion which may once have served to defend Israel's faith and national identity against the threats of syncretism with Canaanite culture and corruption by its fertility religion, but which must now be questionable in our radically different circumstances.

If we disregard the anthropological, social and historical preconceptions that excluded women from the Old Testament priesthood, what are we left with? The idea that the priest and what he offers at the altar must be holy, as God is holy. What we do not have in the Old Testament is any idea that the priest must be male in order to correspond to the maleness of God. The God of the Old Testament is not exclusively male. It is the *perfection* of God which must be mirrored by the perfection of the priest and of the sacrifice. In the thought of the Old Testament male is more perfect

than female in those species, among them humankind,
where there is sexual differentiation; God, however, is
perfect not as male, but as God.

To say that much of the Old Testament is culturally
conditioned is in no way to reduce the importance of its
central insight into the nature of the priesthood. Catholic
Christianity through the ages has understood the distinction
between clergy and laity in terms of the Old Testament idea
of representative holiness, and has thereby been able to
retain that sense of the mysterious nature of the liturgy
through which the sanctity of God and the holy otherness of
worship comes to expression. But equally, Christianity
cannot be content with an Old Testament definition of what
holiness really is. For Jesus himself transformed Judaism at
this very point. The "Holy One of God" (Mark 1:24) was
apparently willing to be defiled by table fellowship with the
unholy. When touched by a haemorrhaging woman in a
crowd – a classic case of Levitical defilement – he did not
complain that he had been contaminated, but enquired who
it was who had drawn sanctifying and healing power from
him (Mark 5:30). For Jesus, it is not defilement but true
holiness which is the greater contagion. In fidelity to his
teaching, Christians have learned to think of holiness in a
more spiritual way. In consequence there is no reason why a
woman cannot be as ritually holy and representatively set
apart for the worship of God, as a man.

The New Testament and Priestly Authority

In the case of the Old Testament material, it was clear that
we were dealing with a recognizable phenomenon of
priesthood. What was less clear was how much of what was
said or assumed there should continue to be influential for
the Church. In the case of the New Testament, the situation
is reversed. The commands of Christ or of the Apostles may
safely be assumed to be influential for the Church, but there
is notoriously no clear reference in the New Testament to a
recognizable institution of Christian priesthood. The early

Church, emerging for its Jewish cradle, issued at first a temporary "no" to the terminology of priesthood, however much we may want to claim that it affirmed a permanent "yes" to the concept of priesthood. It is important to underline this fact because, when we speak of the need to *develop* Church order to allow the priesthood of women today, we are not introducing something unheard of in the tradition. The post-apostolic Church also needed to develop Church order in the first two centuries to allow the institution of a *male* priesthood. Most Christians have been willing to believe that this post-biblical development was inspired by the Holy Spirit, or at least was not totally corrupt. They should not, therefore, find it unthinkable that the Church is being led to accept a similar development in our own day.

In default of any explicit reference in the New Testament to our subject, we are forced back more or less to arguments from analogy. But this type of argument is always difficult to bring under proper control, and in certain recent elaborations it has got out of hand. We propose to consider in turn (a) the argument from analogy with the male priesthood of Christ, (b) the argument from the subordination of women to men in the order of creation, and (c) the argument from Jesus' appointment of twelve men as his apostles. In (a) and (b) the factor of maleness is explicit, but the relevance of the analogies to Christian priesthood is doubtful. In (c) the analogy is much closer and more convincing – there must be some relation between the apostles and the apostolic ministry of the Church – but the question of gender is at best an argument from silence, as we shall see.

(a) A convenient statement of the first kind of argument from analogy may be found in Eric Mascall's contribution to the symposium *Man, Woman and Priesthood*. He writes:

The only ontologically original and ultimate priesthood is that of Christ, it is identical with his status as Son . . . [and] subsists in eternity (Hebrews 4:14 5:5 6:7). Priesthood belongs to Christ as the *Son* of the Father. He became man as male, not by accident, but because he is Son and not Daughter; because what was to be communicated to the created world in human form in the Incarnation was the relation he has to the Father . . . . And because the ordained priest is not exercising a priesthood of his own, but is the agent and instrument through whom Christ is exercising *his* priesthood, he too must be male.[3]

Dr Mascall's insistence that "the only original priesthood is that of Christ" would, not so long ago, have been viewed with some suspicion in his own Anglo-Catholic circles. For, with some such innocent sounding phrase it was customary for Protestant critics to attack the doctrine of eucharistic sacrifice. They argued from the unique priesthood of Christ and the unrepeatable sacrifice of Calvary to the rejection of the Catholic doctrines of ministry and sacraments. In the debates on liturgical revision in the 1960s catholic Anglicans were forced to defend their right to speak of the Church as continuing to offer Christ sacramentally to the Father, and, therefore, of the Church's need for a genuine Christian priesthood in addition to, though in continuity with, the historic priesthood of Christ. Ironically, however, in the current debate on the ordination of women, we hear much less along these lines. This is quite understandable: if the Church has a eucharistic sacrifice and thus a priesthood which is peculiarly her own, and ancillary to the historical sacrifice and priesthood of Jesus, then part at least of the celebrant's role must be to represent the People of God. And since, in ordinary gatherings for worship in this country, the congregation is well over 50 per cent female, it would not be unnatural for a woman to act in that capacity.

It is perhaps to avoid this line of argument, that the notion of the priest as representative has become less popular in recent times than that of the priest as "icon of Christ",[4] implying some sort of visual and external similarity between Christ and the celebrant. But exponents of this approach have never satisfactorily explained why the common possession of human nature is not sufficient "iconic" similarity, or why maleness is essential, while other aspects such as racial and tribal descent, age, circumcision, beard and hairstyle are not. This whole discussion of the priest as visual representation or icon of Christ ought to be treated with extreme caution. For the majority of Christians believe that Christ is really present in the Church's Eucharist, though they may explain that presence in several different ways. Consequently, Christ needs to be made present and "represented" by the celebrant only in a very limited and temporary liturgical sense: and the more important "icon" of Christ in the Eucharist is the sacramental elements, the consecrated bread and wine, to which arguments about the maleness of Christ's earthly humanity simply do not apply.

To return to Mascall's formulation, we should note carefully that the biblical evidence he adduces for the unique priesthood of Christ is drawn exclusively from the Epistle to the Hebrews. This datum, that Christ alone is priest, is crucial for his argument, but it rests on a very slender scriptural base; it is found nowhere else in the New Testament. Hebrews is a brilliantly rhetorical and complex work, and the priesthood of Christ appears within it, *not* as the logical premise for the exposition, but as a deeply paradoxical and rather polemical motif. First, it is paradoxical, inasmuch as the condemned criminal on the cross who suffered a defiling death "outside the camp" (13:11) is viewed, with the eye of faith, as the exact opposite – a perfectly holy priest conducting a ritual of perfect redemption. Secondly, it is polemical, inasmuch as this once-for-all priesthood of Christ renders all other priesthoods, the Levitical in particular, redundant and unnecessary (e.g. 7:11). Furthermore, the only qualification for priesthood which the author of Hebrews grants to the earthly Jesus is his share in our common human nature, excepting only sin. This is emphatically stated (see 2:11, 2:14, 4:15). Thus, if we follow Mascall in his attempt to make the priesthood of Christ in Hebrews the basis of an argument, we shall be forced to the conclusion not that the priesthood of women is illegitimate, but that any kind of priesthood in the Christian Church apart from the historic priesthood of the crucified and risen Saviour is illegitimate. But, of course, to draw either deduction from a christological metaphor would be totally false.

We may leave on one side, as scarcely requiring refutation, Mascall's claim that the eternal Logos is "Son and not Daughter", with all its attendant problems of attributing to the pre-existent Christ not only humanity already, but apparently male human nature! But two other flaws in the interpretation of Hebrews require brief comment. The priesthood of Christ does not "subsist in eternity" in any Platonic sense; it is eternal, not in the sense that it predates the Incarnation, but in the sense that it endures eternally in heaven from now on. In fact, strictly speaking, it post-dates the earthly life of Jesus, for it begins only when the ascended Christ offers the sacrifice of his own blood beyond the veil, "where Jesus has entered on our behalf as forerunner, having become a high priest for ever in the succession of Melchizedek" (6:20). And again, the priesthood of Christ is not "identical with his status as Son", nor does he "communicate to the world the relation he has with the Father". Such ideas derive from the theologies of Paul and John in the New Testament, from which the metaphor of priesthood is absent; it is gratuitous to read them into Hebrews. And the purpose of the priest metaphor in Hebrews has nothing to do with communicating a relationship of sonship but rather with effecting an all-sufficient sacrifice for sin and thus opening up access to God in a clean conscience.

In short, this attempt to use the analogy of the male priesthood of the Incarnate Christ to disallow the priesthood of women must be deemed a failure. The maleness of the human Jesus is not in doubt, but its relevance to his priestly role in Hebrews is nil, and the analogy between that unique priesthood and the forms of later Christian ministry is remote and ultimately even subversive.

(b) The second kind of argument we shall consider works from analogy with the alleged subordination of women to men in the order of creation. It has been expounded by Bishop Graham Leonard in an article[5] which has already been treated to a thorough critical analysis by Anthony Dyson.[6] So it is only necessary here to mention one or two points. According to the Bishop of London, the biblical revelation maintains

> sexual differentiation as part of the divine plan for the creation. Male and female are created to be complementary [and] as Galatians 3:28 makes clear, there are no sex differences in respect of salvation. [Nevertheless] Scripture says that within the redeemed community the relationships between men and women are to be complementary in a way which reflects the fact that there are profound and deep differences between the sexes.[7]

And the author goes on to claim that female subordination is one of these created differences. He ignores the fact that, in Genesis, the subordination of wives to their husbands, along with the pains of childbirth, is explicitly stated to be women's special punishment for the Fall (Gen. 3:16); it is no part of the original plan. Instead, he appeals to the Athanasian Creed[8] to confirm that "subordination does not imply inferiority", either in the case of the second and third persons within the Trinity, or in the case of women in the natural order. This hierarchical principle is then carried over to the issue of an all-male priesthood in the following way:

> It does not surprise me therefore that this ministerial priesthood has been restricted to those who are masculine, i.e. those who psychologically and physically represent because they are men, not because they are virtuous, nor because they have certain abilities, but because they are men. They represent the Divine Initiative, the Divine Begetter.[9]

We do not intend to discuss all the ramifications of this extraordinary statement: the scarcely tenable claim that biological maleness, as such, is sufficient qualification for ordination quite apart from moral qualities and pastoral skills; or the implication that men have by nature a closer affinity to their Creator than women; or the idea that sexual begetting can any longer be understood in terms of male initiative either genetically or psychologically. What we wish simply to point out is that Bishop Leonard is unable to produce a single passage from the New Testament explicitly concerned with the Church's ministry to which his analogy is applicable. In the course of his article, he quotes 1 Cor. 12 as a "paradigm given by nature" of the "pattern of unity and diversity" in the Church. But that passage refers to the possession or lack of spiritual gifts, especially speaking with tongues, and forbids any suggestion of inferiority or subordination, and leaves no room for deep differences between the sexes within the one Body of Christ. He goes on to quote Ephesians 5, where the relations between husband and wife are analogous to those between Christ and the Church; but the ministry is nowhere here in view. What is at issue is the obedience and, it must be admitted, subordination of wives to husbands within the contract of marriage; and the obedience required of children (whether male or female) to their parents, and of slaves to their masters (presumably even of male slaves towards a female master!). It is worth adding that in other less disputed Pauline letters than Ephesians, when the Apostle uses gender-specific metaphors to illuminate the character of his ministry, he never uses the husband – wife analogy. On the contrary, he speaks of himself in the role of marriage-broker at 2 Cor. 11:2, a function which is not exclusively masculine; and even casts himself in the female role of wet-nurse at 1 Thess. 2:7.

We do not wish to imply by this that the Bishop is wrong to see ministry in terms of authority. What we deny is that authority of the appropriate kind, signifying sacramentally the authority of God, and Christ's lordship over the Church, exercised in love, humility and service, has anything to do with natural maleness.

(c) Attempts, such as those analysed above, to render the issue of women's priesthood a theological non-starter fail chiefly because they are unable to demonstrate the relevance of the maleness of the Incarnate Christ, or of the subordinateness of women to men in the story of the Fall to the sex of the ministerial priesthood. They also fail, for other and graver reasons: that they tend to subvert important principles of Christian theology, such as the real presence of Christ in the Eucharist or the supernatural character of the call to sacred priesthood. The third argument from analogy we shall examine is that from Jesus's appointment of twelve men as his inner group of disciples and apostles. This has traditionally been understood as bearing directly on the ordained ministry of the Church, but as we shall see, this approach delivers much less of a knock-down argument than it seems to promise.

First, it should be recognized that we are still in the realm of arguments from analogy. The appointment of the Twelve was not the institution by Jesus of ministerial order, to be handed on by them to likely (male!) successors. The Twelve functioned only for the first Christian generation; apart from the replacement of Judas by Matthias (Acts 1:17), their role was unique to them, and not transferable to others. Thus the selection of men exclusively is not necessarily determinative for later Christian practice. And in fact, there was a special reason, applying solely to the original Twelve, for this preference for men. Apparently, the group of the Twelve were intended to symbolize the reconstitution of Israel in the Last Days, playing the part, as it were, of twelve new Patriarchs or twelve new Elders like those who assisted Moses (Matt. 19:28). The choice of men, therefore, for this unrepeatable eschatological and symbolic function was dictated by the Old Testament parallels. That women, contrary to normal rabbinic custom, figured prominently among the disciples of Jesus is historically a quite remarkable fact about him (Luke 8:1 – 3), and arguably more relevant to the issue of women's ordination.

Secondly, the Twelve were not the only apostles in the early Church; there were others. Apostolic authority for the later priesthood of the Church is not therefore derived through them alone. Paul, for example, based his own claim to apostleship on his vision of the risen Christ (1 Cor. 9:1) and denied that his authority derived by succession from the Twelve at Jerusalem (Gal. 1:15–16). When his opponents raised doubts whether he had the necessary credentials for apostleship (2 Cor. 11:22–33) he replied in terms not of his natural qualifications but of his transcendent call and his solidarity with the sufferings of Christ (2 Cor. 12). There is no hint here that a particular gender was felt to be a prerequisite for such a vocation.[10]

One of the roots of the early Christian concept of an apostle is undoubtedly the teaching of Jesus himself; but Jesus did not limit his "apostles" to adult males only. In his usage the idea was not a technical term referring to office in the Church, but a parable referring to his "business agents" in the world. And he applied the language of agency not only to his disciples (Matt. 10:40) but also to little children (Mark 9:37) who without knowing it bring to bear upon others their principal's rightful claim of love.

The *authority* conferred by Christ on the Twelve and on the apostles of the first generation was inherited, in the later period of the Church's waiting for his delayed Return, by the threefold ordained ministry, and became one of its clearest constitutive features. But it was meant to be a different kind of authority from that commonly found in the structures of this passing age. Jesus himself had distinguished the spiritual authority he wanted his followers to respect from the crude exercise of coercive force typical of the pagan world. "The Kings of the Gentiles exercise lordship over them, and those in authority over them are called Benefactors" – a title favoured by the Ptolemies in Egypt and used popularly in an ironic sense – "but it shall not be so among you" (Luke 22:25). Jesus introduced and exemplified a new kind of authority, real enough in its power of preaching and healing, but in its motivation and manner inseparable from service. This authority, even in the time of Jesus, could be said to have a "priestly" character, for it was typified by sacrifice, by "the Son of Man laying down his life as a ransom for many" (Mark 10:45).

Opponents of women's ordination, like Bishop Leonard, sometimes imply a separation between priestly authority and diaconal service, and allow the latter but not the former to women. Thus he writes: 'The *diakonia*, I believe, is the essentially feminine ministry. . . . This is the one reason I have never had any difficulty about women being deacons."[11] But there is, surely, difficulty in prising apart what Jesus binds so inseparably together: "Whoever would be great among you must be your servant (*'diaconos'*); and whoever would be first among you must be slave of all" (Mark 10:43–4).

This is not at all to empty the notion of authority of any real content, let it be emphasized. Authority is not being reduced to servility; it is indeed an essential constituent of Christian priesthood. For service, pastoral care, counselling and the minstries of word and sacrament are intrinsically authoritative acts, all the more so when the last vestiges of this-worldly authoritarianism are purged from them. Those Christians who have a high regard for priestly authority are understandably wary of any move which might seem to undermine it. They dislike that tendency, more characteristic perhaps of certain segments of the Church of England than of the Roman Catholic or Free Churches in Britain, to treat the ordained ministry as a kind of civil service to the Church. They are possibly afraid that women lack sufficient natural authority to enforce the discipline of Christ in preaching or in the ministry of reconciliation. We believe that their anxieties will quickly prove to be unfounded. The true authority of priesthood is not an innate natural quality, but a supernatural gift, the grace of the Spirit given in ordination; and women priests will in the main, we are confident, exercise an unbureaucratic, genuinely Christian authority, modelled on the sacrificial service of the Son of Man.

Conclusion

As with the earlier discussion of priestly holiness, so with the
theme of priestly authority, study of the biblical evidence
confirms the traditional view that these are vitally important
concepts for the ordained ministry; but at the same time it
reveals that there is within Scripture a process of purification
and transformation of these ideas, such that women as well
as men should rightly be considered capable of symbolizing
and embodying them in the priestly office. We have
attempted to show that the Old Testament exclusion of
women from Israelite priesthood arose from certain
pressures in its environment and from a certain view of what
constitutes human perfection, which was specifically challenged by Jesus himself. Representative and sacramental
holiness remains, but its incidental link with a particular
gender has been severed. We have attempted similarly to
show that arguments from analogy, which employ pieces of
biblical evidence to justify excluding women from the
Christian priesthood, fail to make their case, and sometimes
in the process threaten basic principles of Christian faith.
Ministerial and sacrificial authority remains, and a proper
appreciation of its true nature will lead not to the rejection
but to the positive acceptance of women as priests.

*This chapter first appeared as a booklet published in 1984 by the
Movement for the Ordination of Women.*

NOTES

1. The 'Lima' text, *Baptism, Eucharist and Ministry* (Geneva,
   WCC, 1982, p. 24) notes that ''an increasing number of
   churches have decided that there is no biblical or

theological reason against ordaining women''. In the attached *Commentary*, p. 25, however, it adds that those who oppose women's ordination ''believe that there are theological issues concerning the nature of humanity and concerning Christology which lie at the heart of their convictions''. This is a rather stronger statement than is to be found in the recent bilateral dialogue, *Anglican-Roman Catholic Commission: The Final Report*, (London, CTS/SPCK, 1982, p. 44): the Commission ''believes that the principles upon which its doctrinal agreement rests are not affected by such ordinations [of women]; for it was concerned with the origin and nature of the ordained ministry and not with the question who can or cannot be ordained''. In other words, the exclusion of women from priesthood is more a matter of ecclesiastical discipline than of theology.

2. See further, Mary Hayter, *The New Eve in Christ: The Use and Abuse of the Bible in the Debate about Women in the Church* (London: SPCK, 1987) pp. 69–70).

3. ''Some Basic Considerations'', pp. 22–3 (author's emphasis) in *Man Woman and Priesthood*, ed. P.L. Moore (London: SPCK, 1978).

4. See K. Ware, ''Man, Woman and the Priesthood of Christ'', pp. 79–83, in *op. cit.,* n.3 above. Compare also the critique of the way the notion of icon is used in this connection by G.A. Muddiman, ''The Priesthood of Women'', in *Kairos,* Vol. 6 (Oxford: St Stephen's House, 1982) pp. 18–21.

5. ''The Ordination of Women: Theological and Biblical Issues'', in *Epworth Review*, xi, January 1984, pp. 42–9.

6. A.O. Dyson, ''Dr Leonard on the Ordination of Women'', in *Theology*, lxxxvii, March 1984, pp. 87–95.

7. *Art. Cit.* p. 43.

8. He continues, rather curiously (p. 44): ''The word *hypostasis* is, as is well known, not in scripture, but the word *hypostasso* [sic]) from which it derives is.'' He is presumably referring to the well known fact that the *homoousios* of the Nicene Creed does not appear in

scripture. But neither *hypostasis* nor *homoousios* has any connection with the verb *hypotasso*, ''I subject'' or ''subordinate''.

9. *Art. cit.* p. 49.
10. It is even possible that the original text of Romans 16:17 refers to a *female* apostle in the early Church.
11. *Art. cit.* p. 48.

5

Eucharistic Presidency

John Austin Baker

What is it specifically about blessing, absolving and celebrating the Eurcharist which means that they cannot be performed by a woman? Why indeed should it be these three tasks, of all others, which cause so much concern? Are they not, after all, ones which depend least on our own human qualities? We indignantly repudiate any suggestion that the effectiveness of a blessing or the forgiveness mediated through absolution has anything at all to do with us: it is God who blesses and forgives. The power is all from him. Likewise, there is not a single authoritative Christian understanding of the Eucharist which suggests that it is the quality of the minister which controls the grace. On the contrary, in the classic phrase: "the unworthiness of the minister hindereth not the effect of the sacrament". It is Christ who comes to his people of his own divine charity, and the Holy Spirit which unites us with him through the receiving of the elements, and all as the gift of the Father's eternal will to save and redeem his creatures. No accomplishments are required to preside at this sacred interchange except the ability to say the words in which the Church prays to God for this grace and to perform the simple actions involved. By contrast, other ministerial activities, such as teaching, preaching, counselling and pastoral care, all palpably require human capacities of one sort or another which are not necessarily found in everyone.

Ironically, of course, teaching, preaching, counselling and

pastoral care and activities which have been widely entrusted
to women in, for example, the Church of England, which is
divided on whether or not to admit them to perform the
three priestly functions. This makes it impossible to rule out
the ordination of women on the grounds that the eucharistic
presidency should be confined to those officially exercising a
pastoral and teaching ministry, since women already do this.
Any decisive objection must be rooted, therefore, in the
nature of the priestly state or the priestly actions themselves.
To carry such theological weight, priesthood cannot be, as
some would regard it, a secondary matter of "good order
and godly discipline", but has to be seen as an integral part
of the great mystery of faith, a revelation and mediation of
God's love in creation, incarnation, death and resurrection,
and in harmony with everything else we know of these
things. In other words, holy order as at present received
becomes an essential element in tradition, and any change is
a change in the heart of Christian faith and experience.

Part of Christian tradition is undeniably that, until recent
times, it was the universal practice of the Church to restrict
ordination to men; and today it is still the practice of very
much the larger part of Christendom. But this fact is seen as
important not primarily as a truth about Church practice
but as witness to something deeper, namely a particular
understanding of God's salvation. If we truly respond to
God's will for us, the argument runs, we shall see that for
women to preside at the Eucharist is contrary to the divine
order in the world and in redemption. Society today may be
out of tune with that divine will and order, but that makes it
all the more necessary that the Church should not defect
from it. The key to God's will is to be found in the fact that
the eternal Son of God became human as a man; and what
matters is the link between this truth and the eucharistic
presidency.

If this is our perspective on the question, then the change
involved in ordaining women to the priesthood, so far from
being marginal or minimal, will be massive and could be
disastrous. Those who argue for such ordination, therefore,

cannot rest content with a purely pragmatic case. They have to engage seriously with the argument from tradition; and this of course they have sought to do, citing, for example, the words of Genesis, where the image of God in human beings is something given to us as creatures who include both male and female; the striking place of women in the Gospels; St Paul's dictum that "in Christ there is neither male nor female", and so on. In other words, they are saying that the tradition is not monolithic, even in its origins. Turning to later times, they point to the leading and influential part that women have played in Christian history, often against the whole tendency of society at large: as heads, founders and reformers of religious orders; as mystics and teachers of spirituality; as missionaries and pioneers of every kind of active charity; as theologians, and as advisers to those in high places in the Church; in Eastern Orthodoxy as Christian rulers, counted worthy even of the title *isapostolos*, "equal of the apostles". At the same time, criticisms are made of the tradition on the grounds that it has often been distorted by the unthinking adoption of the values of the secular world with regard to the relative positions of men and women, in particular that it displays unhealthy psychological features of an immature male fear of women or aggressive suppression of them. In this connection there has grown up in recent years a radical and at times violent critique of Christianity from the standpoint of the feminist movement, and in certain of its exponents this has led to a desire to transform the religion, especially in its idea of God, out of all recognition.

In all these ways the movement for the ordination of women has had to probe far deeper than mere reform of the institutional structures of the Church, and wrestle with fundamental matters of faith. But this raises another very important question. If we approach the tradition with one specific issue in mind, and if we ask it questions about that issue alone, we are liable to begin to misinterpret it. We may fall into the trap of supposing that our particular concern, in this case the place of women, has controlled its development far more widely than it really has. To take one obvious example: resistance to ordaining women to the priesthood in many cases takes its rise not from any theological reflection about women at all, but from a particular theology of the Eucharist which has developed without any reference to women or men as such.

It is not without significance that ordination of women as ministers began in Protestant denominations whose theology of the Eurcharist was radically different from that which had evolved in Catholic Christianity. When representatives of the latter school say that the Reformation Churches do not ordain ministers as sacrificing priests, they are, of course, quite right; and any objections based on this sacrificial understanding of the Eucharist will seem quite irrelevant to those who regard it differently. Can the two sides, therefore, enter into meaningful discussion of what women may or may not do in the Church, until they have resolved their differences about the Eucharist?

In this connection it is interesting to remember the reactions to the report of ARCIC I on the Eucharist. What that report offered was a creative restatement of eucharistic doctrine in which both the Roman Catholic and Anglican members of the Commission could see something better and more positive than the formulas of the past, something which enabled each side to discover in a larger synthesis the partial truths which they had cherished, and to enrich them with new truths from other sources. While some welcomed this, there were those on both sides who rejected it because it had abandoned the words they were accustomed to use, and therefore must be regarded as contaminating the pure truth as they had been taught to believe it. This may perhaps be one reason why Rome has been guarded and even cool towards the work of the Commission, and why on the Anglican side, too, various provinces of the Anglican Communion voiced strong preliminary reservations. The view has also been expressed that Rome, knowing that women had been ordained as priests in some parts of the Anglican Communion, and foreseeing that they soon would be in others, was negative towards ARCIC because it seemed both unkind and pointless to raise false hopes by approving the statements on Eucharist and Ministry when the door would have to be slammed shut later for other reasons. If this were true, it would only illustrate the point that in these documents the issues discussed were not those of women's ordination at all, but rather questions of the nature of the Eucharist itself. In fact, there are real and profound differences of conviction about the nature of the Eucharist which the prophetic inspiration of the ARCIC members has so far been unable to heal. This has undoubtedly had practical consequences in the debate about women's ordination. But the eucharistic controversy is a difference of tradition in its own right, and should be respected as such.

This may be tackled in two different ways. One is to pursue the line followed by Commissions such as ARCIC, and work for a consensus on the Eucharist. Some real progress on this has been made on a world scale by the World Council of Churches, as evidenced by the Lima document, *Baptism, Eucharist and Ministry*, which is being discussed at parish and congregational level all over the world. Since a large number of the Churches in the WCC do ordain women to their ministries, this clearly could be one way forward, even if a slow one. A rather different and more direct route, however, is to ask whether women's ordination is ruled out *even on the traditional Catholic view of the sacrament of the Eucharist*.

Both Roman Catholic and Eastern Orthodox theology teach that in the Eucharist the elements of bread and wine do truly and indeed become the body and blood of Christ, though Eastern theologians have not usually accepted the technical, philosophical explanation of this in terms of transubstantiation. To simplify matters, let us concentrate on the Roman Catholic eucharistic doctrine which is the most influential in the West among those who disagree with women's ordination on grounds of sacramental theology.

Put briefly, the dynamics of the Eucharist on this view are

as follows. The priest, on behalf of the whole church, prays to God the Father that the bread and wine on the altar may become for us the body and blood of Christ, citing as his authority for this prayer the words of Jesus at the Last Supper, when he said of the bread "this is my body" and of the wine "this is my blood", and commanded us to do this as a memorial of him. By his actions and words on this occasion the Lord identified the sacramental bread and wine with his body broken and blood shed upon the cross; and thus in the Eucharist it is that sacrificial offering which is made present when God the Father grants our prayer and by the power of the Holy Spirit causes the miraculous transformation to take place. It is not correct to say, as Protestant critics of Roman theology used to do, that Christ is believed to be sacrificed again at every mass. The sacrifice of Calvary was indeed once for all but, because the broken body and outpoured blood are made truly present in the eucharistic elements, that one sacrifice is realized again in our midst and its saving power invoked for our salvation. That is why that Christian tradition speaks not just of the holy table but of the altar. The one altar where the sacrifice was offered by Christ was the cross but, because in human worship the place of sacrifice is traditionally called an altar, in Catholic spirituality the place where Christ's sacrifice is made present is also called an altar; and likewise the person who offers the prayer in answer to which God makes the sacrifice present is called a "priest", because that is what sacred persons who officiate at sacrifices have always been called.

Why, however, even on this understanding of the Eucharist, need there be any objection to the ordination of women as priests? What the celebrant does is to ask God the Father by the power of the Holy Spirit to make Christ and his sacrifice present in the bread and wine which are themselves the gift to us of the Father's love in creation. Everything is done by God the holy Trinity; and above all the sacrifice is performed totally by Christ, because it is his self-offering on Calvary to his Father which is made present

among us – not anything at all that we do. The place, if we
may use that word, in which his offering of himself becomes
real here and now is in the bread and wine on the altar. It is
by eating and drinking these that Christ's body and blood
are received.

As a consequence, the liturgical action itself is also
described as a sacrifice. The priest says to the congregation,
"Pray, brethren, that my sacrifice and yours may be
acceptable to God the Almighty Father"; and the people
respond, "May the Lord accept the sacrifice at your hands
for the praise and glory of his name, for our good, and the
good of all his Church." It is true the sacrifice which the
priest "offers" liturgically to God, the ritual act, is
understood as worthy only because the substance and heart
of it, the offering that is made, is the one perfect sacrifice
completed by our Lord outside Jerusalem 1,950 years ago,
and which itself represented in earthly terms the perfect love
and devotion of the eternal Son to the Father within the holy
Trinity.

The question, therefore, needs to be pressed: why, on this
understanding of the Eucharist, does the celebrant have to
be a man? Surely all that is necessary is that the priest should
be an officially appointed representative of the Church? In
fact, the argument for the necessity of a male representative
does not draw on this central theology of the eucharistic
sacrifice so much as on a secondary elaboration of it, which
has grown up over the centuries.

To trace the historical development of this elaboration
would be a delicate and complex task, but perhaps its logical
structure can be presented more concisely. If the sacrifice
which saved the world was Christ's offering of himself to
God in his death on Calvary; and if that is complete once for
all, and nothing we do can add to it; then, when the body
and blood are made miraculously present on the altar, it is
that one perfect and complete self-offering of Christ which is
present in them. At the same time the priest, by prayer and
action, presents that perfect and complete sacrifice of Christ
before the Father, and therefore can in a sense be said to

offer Christ's sacrifice to God the Father. In the same way, devotion can speak of the liturgy as *our* sacrifice: the sacrifice offered to God by the people of God, through their authorized representative, is Christ's sacrifice, which God gives us to offer to himself. But piety telescoped this cumbrous precision to say that the priest offers Christ's sacrifice to the Father. Almost inevitably, therefore, the point at which the offering is made comes to be thought of not as Calvary, miraculously recreated by God within the bread and wine, which is something invisible and difficult to grasp, but as the visible moment when the priest says the words of Christ and holds up the host to be adored.

Such language would, of course, be intolerable if it were taken to imply that the human minister in his own person offered Christ. There is, therefore, great spiritual pressure to think of Christ as present not just in the bread and wine but also in the sacred minister himself. If this is when Christ is "offered" to the Father, then it must be Christ in some miraculous way who makes the offering. The priest, utterly unworthy as he is, becomes for that moment Christ himself, as truly as the mundane bread and wine become Christ's body and blood. The priest is *alter Christus*, a "second Christ". But if this is the way the invisible truth of the matter is conceived, it becomes psychologically very difficult to be at ease with a woman performing this liturgical function.

Another rather different line of thought which may well contribute to the same psychological difficulty is that which sees the Eucharist as a re-enactment of the Last Supper. This is something which may well be deeply, if unconsciously, embedded in Church of England piety. In the Book of Common Prayer we have the arrangement of the Eucharist which represented Cranmer's final thoughts in his revision of 1552. Here the prayer of consecration stops immediately after the words of institution. Once the priest has said, "Do this, as oft as ye shall drink it, in remembrance of me", the worshippers proceed straight to the communion. In other words, it is as if they were in the upper room and Jesus was saying those words for the first time and they, like the disciples, were receiving the bread and wine from his hands.

In our modern liturgies this dramatic reconstruction has been rightly abandoned. The Eucharist is not a repetition of the Last Supper. We are living in the world after the cross and resurrection and the coming of the Holy Spirit. What at the Last Supper was a salvation still to be achieved, has been achieved and bestowed and we are giving thanks for it, which is what Eucharist means. The remembrance we make is not of the Last Supper but of Christ's suffering and victory which we remember before God as a prayer for the final and complete coming of the Kingdom. But Cranmer suppressed that aspect of the Eucharist: even in the prayer of thanksgiving after the communion he mentions only the cross, leaving out the resurrection and ascension which were in his medieval models.

All this has now been handsomely restored; and in this respect the new services are theologically a great improvement. But, among older church members at any rate, the Last Supper interpretation of the Eucharist could still be a powerful background influence; and, by a quirk of history, the present popularity of the westward position for the celebrant, making him so visually reminiscent of the figure of Christ in pictures of the Last Supper, may well create the same image of the priest in the minds of those for whom the 1662 Book is unknown territory. If, therefore, the worshippers do consciously or unconsciously associate the celebrant with Christ at the Last Supper, it could again seem to them highly inappropriate to suggest that a woman should take that place.

To return, however, to the central Catholic theology of the Eucharist, the essential core of this is as follows: ''. . . in the bountiful sacrament of the holy Eucharist, after the consecration of the bread and wine, our Lord and Saviour Jesus Christ, true God and man, is contained truly, really and substantially under the appearance of the objects that the senses can perceive . . . by that form of existence which is possible to God, though we can hardly express it in words" (Council of Trent, Decree concerning the Most Holy Eucharist, c. 1). In short, *it is in the consecrated elements that Christ is present to be adored and to be received* in the supremely real mode peculiar to the Eucharist alone. This miracle is wholly the work of God.

But what of the sacred minister? Pope Paul VI quotes the famous words of St John Chrysostom: "It is not the man who is responsible for the offerings becoming Christ's body and blood, it is Christ himself. . . . The standing figure belongs to the priest who speaks these words, the power and the grace belong to God. 'This is my body,' he says; this sentence transforms the offerings." (Encyclical Letter, *Mysterium Fidei*, 1965, para. 49). The Second Vatican Council teaches: ". . . Christ is always present in His Church, especially in her liturgical celebrations. He is present in the sacrifice of the Mass, not only in the person of His minister, 'The same one now offering, through the ministry of priests, who formerly offered himself on the cross' [Council of Trent, ibid., c. 2], but especially under the Eucharistic species" (Consitution on the Sacred Liturgy, *Sacrosanctum Concilium*, c. 7). Again: "Through the ministry of priests, the spiritual sacrifice of the faithful is made perfect in union with the sacrifice of Christ, the sole Mediator. Through the hands of priests and in the name of the whole Church, the Lord's sacrifice is offered in the Eucharist in an unbloody and sacramental manner until He himself returns" (Decree on the Ministry and Life of Priests, *Presbyterorum Ordinis*, 2). Again: ". . . priests must instruct them [namely the faithful] to offer to God the Father the divine Victim in the sacrifice of the Mass, and to join to it the offering of their own lives" (ibid., c. 5). The thrust of these passages may be summed up as follows. The power and grace of God alone effect the miracle of the Eucharist. The sacrifice offered is Christ's, and he alone can offer it. The instruments through which God's grace and Christ's love for the Father work the miracle in the liturgy are the hands and voice of the priest. *But the miracle which is worked is to make Christ truly present in the bread and the wine.*

In *Mysterium Fidei* Pope Paul VI lists various ways in which Christ is present in his Church: at prayer, in works of mercy, in daily living, in preaching, in apostolic governance, and in the administration of the sacraments, supremely the sacrifice of the mass. This and all sacraments are Christ's actions, and he administers them by the agency of men (paras. 35–8). It is clear that this agency is not confined in all cases to ordained men, since in case of necessity a lay woman can administer baptism and it is still the action of Christ. Is there any theological reason why his action in the Eucharist should not take place through the agency of any duly ordained and authorized member of the people of God, which as a whole "offers to God the Father the divine Victim in the sacrifice of the Mass", whether that member be man or woman?

Such agents are representatives not representations of Christ. The liturgy of St John Chrysostom has some relevant words on this subject: "There are some who say: I wish to see Christ and His Face and His Features and His Clothing and His Sandals. But here in the Eucharist you see Him, you touch Him, you eat Him. . . . It was not enough for him to become simply one man. . . . He mingles himself with ourselves and makes us his Body, not just by faith but in truth and reality" (*Liturgy of St John Chrysostom*, Prayer at the Little Entrance, quoted in *The Thyateira Confession*, 1975).

An iconic theory of the eucharistic presidency, confining that role to someone of the same gender as the incarnate Lord, runs the risk of suggesting that Christ is present and active in the eucharistic minister in a unique mode and degree, an idea for which there is no basis in the general doctrine of grace or in specific authoritative teaching. By so doing it obscures the central affirmation of Catholic eucharistic theology, that Christ and his sacrifice are contained and communicated within the consecrated elements, and that that is where his people are to find, adore and receive him. Furthermore, it blurs the nature of the Eucharist by presenting it as a re-enactment of the Last Supper, rather than a fulfilment of the command there given to plead the sacrifice of the cross before God by the sacramental means proleptically provided.

These are serious distortions of Catholic belief. To admit women to the order of priesthood is the straightforward way to remedy them and to promote a truer Catholic tradition. If the only objections to so doing are the very distortions themselves, is not this the course which that tradition actually demands of us?

This chapter first appeared as an article in Theology, *September 1985, pp. 350–7.*

6

The Way Things Change

Pia Buxton

I am a spiritual director; my experience in ministry is chiefly that of listening to what happens to people when they pray, when they recognize God in their lives. And in this work I am repeatedly reminded that questions and doubts can be an essential part of the movement towards change and growth.

I want to explore three kinds of questions currently being asked about the Roman Catholic Church's practice of restricting ordination to men. First, there is the very practical issue of whether the present structure is working; are there not indications of serious problems in our authority and sacramental systems? I call these operational doubts. Then there is the question of whether present practice is true to the heart of the Christian faith; did Jesus mean it to be like this and does the Holy Spirit inspire its continuance? These I call ideological doubts. And, thirdly, there are ethical doubts about the Church's failure to comply with its own teaching on justice and equality for women.

As I see it, these kinds of doubt arise as a healthy corrective to and criticism of the way in which the Christian vision has become fixed and static. I find it helps to illustrate the positive role of these doubts and questions with a model (see page 62).

Imagine the original myth, the root story of Christianity, the life, death and resurrection of Jesus: the story that is not only THEN but also our life source among us NOW in our faith and memories, generating the incarnation among us

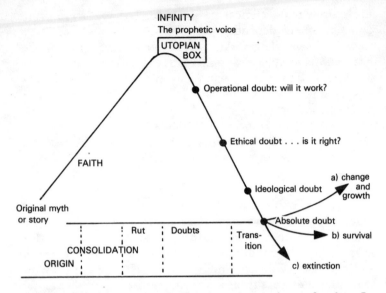

and inspiring the truly Christ-centred questions of today. In attempting to live out that myth the Church as an organization has experienced stages of formation, consolidation and stabilization during which there has, at times, emerged a mistaking of the journey for the arrival. The Utopian flaw, a defended box that resists change and in which the vision of yesterday becomes fixed, arises when leaders cannot face the tension between spontaneity and structure, between creativity and format. We all succumb to the Utopian flaw at times, thinking perfection is all there in the box, nicely preserved and not to be disturbed. But although we need the box for our stability, we also need the disturbing voice of the prophetic call so often engendered by the questions and doubts of the contemplative praying the Gospels in freedom and hope.

Is the Present Structure Working?

In the Roman Catholic Church both the teaching authority and the sacramental system come down from the top to the bottom of a hierarchical pyramid through channels which are entirely male, clerical and celibate. The sharing of Word and Sacrament depends upon the numbers and quality of male, celibate clergy. At each level of the hierarchy the channels have to be strong, lively, alert, speaking relevantly and clearly if they are to win the respect both of those on the next step down and of the vast majority of Church members on the base-line.

There are two respects in which the present structure is not working well. Increasingly those at the base-line are educated, expectant of equality between the sexes and of making their voices heard. This is especially true of women (who make up 60 per cent of the base-line) and is most true of women religious who constitute the largest, most bonded, group of articulate women in the Church today, possessing years of experience in pastoral care and organization as well as degrees and doctorates in theology. From both women and men there is doubt and questioning down on the base-line and some way up the pyramid.

Secondly, in most parts of the world, perhaps for reasons divinely inspired, there is a shortage of younger clergy. This unhealthy, top-heavy age structure has serious implications for the quality and numbers of those manning the pyramid. In this situation there seems to be three possible responses. The system could stay much the same but with fewer and fewer clergy being more and more stretched to cover the ground and becoming increasingly overworked. Secondly, we could develop a less sacramental, less authoritarian Church placing greater emphasis on other aspects like Gospel and prayer which are open to all. (The Church is perhaps at its most vital where groups pray together around the Gospel.) Or, thirdly, we could open up and share out the ministries, decreasing their entrenchment in rite, law and sharply defined roles. For, after all, isn't ministry the sharing with others of what we ourselves value? I think we need a minimizing of order and a maximizing of ministry.

The problems and weaknesses of the present system are not obvious to everyone; systems do not break down suddenly, they teeter about and people get hurt and lost while the law is kept but the service suffers. And not many people who are being overworked really have time to contemplate and reflect; under pressure there is not time to keep in touch with and be touched by the myth and to recognize the mystery in our lives and the world around. When we are over-stretched we tend to look at the machinery and the organization instead of the Good News, which is like suggesting that a sea-sick passenger should spend a little time in the engine room. But the Church is about hearing and sharing the Good News and everything else is simply a means to that end.

Is the Present Practice True to the Heart of the Christian Faith?

Whatever the Good News is, it is with us *now*; it is a constant received by people within their own time and place. And so today questions are rightly being asked about the exclusion of women from ordination. Did Jesus mean it to be like this? Does the Holy Spirit inspire its continuance? When venerable tradition is cited as a reason for the non-ordination of women we need to ask questions of tradition. Does it derive from the example of Jesus? Does it reveal sound doctrine? Can it be changed?

So, *does* the Church's current teaching derive from the example of Jesus? In His relationship with women and what He asked of them in ministry, Jesus acted against the culture and customs of His time to a quite extraordinary degree and to such an extent that clear signs of it have come through into the Gospels despite male censorship in the early Church. He broke the barriers of prejudice, declared Himself Lord of the Sabbath, and went to those in need offering them freedom of spirit in place of the oppressive structures and limiting expectations of their normal role. He broke out of the Utopian Flaw in ways which have since been erased or ignored. I believe Jesus spoke out of a male and female understanding, used masculine and feminine imagery, acting with empathy for both sexes and towards a fullness of humanity. Jesus called women to ministries which are denied them today, allowing women to minister to himself along with the angels, and calling them to a fullness of mission through their ministry. He commended Mary of Bethany for taking up the traditional position of a disciple, seated, listening at the master's feet, a position then reserved for men only. He revealed two essential features of His messianic identity to women; at Jacob's well to the Samaritan woman, and to Martha: ''I am the resurrection . . .'' to which she, not Peter, made reply: ''You are the Christ, the Son of God . . .'' Jesus sent Mary Magdala out from the garden with the most important message of Christianity on the first Easter morning. To be sent by Jesus, as Jesus was sent by the Father, is to be an Apostle.

We teach that the miracles and parables foretell the sacraments. Women anointed Jesus's head and His feet; Mary bore and fed Him, only a woman had the ability to give body and blood to make the Word incarnate; no body, no Eucharist. And then there is the woman seeking her lost coin in the very centre of the repentance and forgiveness parables. It is natural for women to feed, to heal, to anoint and make whole. We do not know if there were any women at the last supper, the celebration of the eucharistic meal, but certainly they were more in evidence than the men at the Eucharistic sacrifice.

Of tradition we must also ask whether it reveals sound doctrine and whether it can change. Let me quote a little from Newman's *Essay on the Development of Christian Doctrine*.[1]

From the nature of the human mind, time is necessary for the full comprehension and perfection of great ideas; and that the highest and most wonderful truths, though communicated to the world once for all by inspired teachers, could not be comprehended all at once by the recipients, but, as being received and transmitted by minds not inspired and through media which were human, have required only longer time and deeper thought for their full elucidation. This may be called the 'Theory of the Development of Doctrine''. (pp. 21 – 2)

In a higher world it is otherwise, but here below to live is to
change, and to be perfect is to have changed often. (p. 30)

No one doctrine can be named which starts complete at
first, and gains nothing afterwards from the investigations
of faith and the attacks of heresy. The Church went forth
from the old world in haste, as the Israelites from Egypt
"with their dough before it was leavened, their kneading
troughs being bound up in their clothes upon their
shoulders". (p. 50)

Is the Present System Right?

Finally, there are the ethical doubts about the Church's
refusal to comply with its own teaching on justice and
equality for women. Is it right that only ordained men
should consecrate, absolve and preach? And is it right that
the whole structure of governance and authority be male,
clerical and celibate? There is a contradiction here between
present practice and our Church's explicit statements about
the rights of women. Let me quote one such statement:

> With respect to the fundamental rights of the person every
> type of discrimination, whether social or cultural, whether
> based on sex, race, colour, social condition, language or
> religion, is to be overcome and eradicated as contrary to
> God's intent. For in truth, it must be regretted that
> fundamental personal rights are not being universally
> honoured; such is the case of women who are denied the
> rights of freedom . . . to embrace a state of life, or to
> acquire an education or benefits equal to those recognised
> for men . . . (GS 29)

And, as *Pacem in Terris* recommends, those who find they
have rights have the responsibility to claim them. That was a
very risky recommendation! When we talk about rights and
Church structures our primary concern is with the right and
responsibility to bring the feminine up into the fullness of

ministry in the Church; it is beneficial to the Church as a whole that women have a voice in governing and a share in its teaching authority. To many women and men the ordination of women seems essential if the Catholic Church is to be credible to those who take seriously issues of justice and inclusiveness. We are members of a very masculine Church in a world whose patterns, models and expectations are mostly given from the male point of view. I believe that if women were to have equality of voice and some real influence in the Church we would begin to see quite new patterns of authority, ministry and worship which would inform and be informed by a new hearing of the Word of God.

The Future

Human consciousness, at its best, is universally growing towards a sense of the global, has a longing for wholeness, for relatedness, for sensitivity to person rather than achievment among things. I suggest that some of the important movements of our time, the peace movement, the ecological movement, holistic spirituality and even ecumenism, are expressions of this and that they are quite radically feminine, often much more so than the feminist movement itself. By their biological role and through their experience women are made for the sustaining of life, for close human relationship, for nurturing very small dreams and beginnings into matter, for incarnating fragility and for holding life in being through relating to it. Paul Tournier suggests that ". . . Our world is masculine, and dominated by masculine values . . . objectivity, achievement, reason and competition . . . this situation has given rise to enormous contrast between the great powers of science and technology and the decline in the quality of life; men have constructed a world of things in which people suffer; this is a situation in which women can make a vital contribution; they have had to struggle and adapt to a masculine society; now they must cure our civilization of its sickness by introducing what is missing, a sense of person."[2] I believe women have a corrective to bring to the Church; their ordination might be a part of that.

Nearly 400 years ago the foundress of my congregation, Mary Ward, endeavoured to obtain for her sisters a new form of apostolic religious life in which enclosure was not bestowed upon them by the decree of men, but in which they governed themselves by the appointment of their own superior general, adopted a rule, the constitution of the Society of Jesus, and lived it as women. She said, ". . . there is no such difference between men and women that women may not do great things, and as I hope will be seen in time to come women will do much . . ." In her time this was not accepted; my forebears were unkindly called Jesuitesses, gadabouts and galloping girls. Now we have become respectable and of worldwide distribution, we are called the Institute of the Blessed Virgin Mary. It took 300 years to have Mary Ward approved as our foundress and 370 years to obtain the constitution she had chosen.

Perhaps we should not expect rapid change on an issue as far reaching as the ordination of women in a Church so large and international, but there are changes in the Church's attitude, there are signs that the Church is hearing and reflecting feminine influences in the world around it. There are for example, new models of the Church beside the institutional one. I'm always thinking up new ones; the listening Church; the gossiping Church (meaning of course the visiting and verbal encouragement by midwives as they gossiped new life into being) and so on.

Very large tankers cannot turn rapidly, very big animals change course slowly but when the eyes begin to move and the head begins to turn it is of the nature of things that the body will follow. During, and after, Vatican 2 there was great change in the Church and an extraordinary ability for the bulk of the faithful to move with willingness and even joy; between one Sunday and the next we could hardly recognize ourselves. I suggest we keep working at this question of the ordination of women, seeking to bring the gifts of the truly feminine up into the life of the Church, helping to develop a fully human community.

From a talk given at the Roman Catholic-Anglican Conference at Heythrop College on 21 March, 1987.

NOTES

1. H. Newman, *An Essay on the Development of Christian Doctrine* (London: Sheed & Ward, 1960) pp. 21–2.
2. P. Tournier, *The Gift of Feeling* (London: SCM, 1980).

7

Self-Awareness in the Image of God

Alexina Murphy

I am going to speak very personally about our understanding of God. I like the phrase sometimes used, "God
talk". How do we talk about God? What language do we
use? What do we say of God? Where does our knowledge of
God come from? How do we learn more about God? How
do we know we are on the right track? How do we share
what we know? "God talk" necessarily says something
about myself, something about my neighbour and then
something about God. The more I can say about myself, the
more self-knowing I am, the more I have to bring to an
awareness of God. Scripture could not be more direct and
emphatic about the importance of loving our neighbour
whom we do see, if we are desirous of loving our God whom
we do not see. Religion is relationships. Growing up in a
family, getting married and raising a family supplies us with
a wealth of experience of relationship which furnish the
language and images of our religion.

The question I want to address, is where does our self-
identity as a person come from? We are told that as new
babies each of us learns the boundaries between self and
mother; to begin with we do not know the difference.
Gradually our self-awareness comes from the family and the
wider circle into which we are born. Our intelligence and
our imagination forges meaning from what we see and hear
outside ourselves and what we discover in our own deep-
seated feelings. We learn what it is to be a human being and

how to relate. We learn that men and women are not the same and locate ourselves according to our gender. As we grow and gain a larger experience, so our notions of self and other are developed, refined and transformed. We are drawing our identity into ourselves from the people and culture around us, working on this within our own personality centre, evaluating what we are learning and to some extent exercising choice over whom we wish to become.

Whether female or male, we draw into our understanding the generally held view of what is appropriate to women and men. The first thing we want to know about a new baby is what sex it is. Our response to a person of the same sex and to individuals of the opposite sex, even when they are still new babies, is influenced both by who they are and who we think they ought to be according to what is expected of a man or a woman. Most of us can distinguish differences in the way we feel about our mother on the one hand and our father on the other, about our sister and our brother. As parents in our turn, we find ourselves responding differently to sons and to daughters. Different facets of ourselves are evoked by the individuality of our children (as it was by our parents and siblings) which always includes an interplay of my sex and theirs. As I know myself and am in relation to persons of the same sex, I am the subject of my experience. In meeting persons of the opposite sex, I am in encounter with the other. I have to allow that my experience as a woman is not the same as a man's. I am the subject of being a female human being but male humanity is the object of my knowing. Conversely, women are the object of men's knowing. If we think of God as exclusively male, behave as if God is the subject but never the object of male behaviour, as if God is never the subject of female behaviour, but always the object, then we never really grapple with the truth that God does not have gender and sexuality. When we think of God in personal terms, we have to attribute gender to God, since we do not know any person without their being either male or female. But we must also be aware that gender and sexuality are human realities in which we are like, but not the same as God. If we assume that God is male, we soon behave as if the male is God.

As well as messages about gender and sexuality, we receive assumptions about authority and good government, about right and wrong, about the good life. Some general notion of where it all comes from (from God who created us) and where it all leads to (heaven when we die) is part of what we have acquired before we begin to reflect consciously on what we know and what we stand for. As a cradle Catholic, I know that growing up in a committed Christian family, going to a Catholic school, learning history in a Christian Catholic bias, was profoundly formative of my sense of who I am and what the world is. Growing up British, in wartime, in a white skin, of professional middle-class folk, affected all my values. Without conscious effort on my part, I acquired notions of God as Father, Son and Spirit, of creation and fall, of incarnation and redemption and resurrection, of Church and priest, of Mary our mother and still a Virgin, of Joseph her chaste spouse, of the divine infant, of the devil, the world and the flesh. In other words enough baggage for anyone to unpack in one lifetime. You won't be surprised that I assumed God was male; when he chose to come among us, he became a man after all. The man Jesus always addressed God – so we understand from Scripture – as Father. Jesus continues to be present with us in His Mystical Body. Tangled up together are attributions of gender and embodiment, which leaves the notion of a soul, which I forgot to mention, floating without either. At a deeper level, God is an inextricable element in both self and other, permeating all the boundaries of awareness. So how do we go about unscrambling these coded messages?

As an adult looking back over twenty or thirty years, I can see certain significant shifts in my consciousness of who God is. I can remember being at mass on a Sunday, probably twenty years ago, with three small children and a new baby. Our Father . . . we prayed. I can remember thinking: ''My God!'' If God feels half as weighed down with responsibility as I do, half as harrassed with clamorous demands from unreasonable children as I do, we should be praying for God. My predicament was that however well-informed and well-intentioned one is as a parent, we can hardly ever get it right for the children but we expect God our Father to get it right for us. At that point, I stopped being a child in relation to God who is father, the indulgent parent who makes it all come out right in the end. I had a new respect for God, perhaps a better sense of distance from God. At some level of consciousness, I felt equal to God, in a peer relationship with God as creator and redeemer. I felt myself more of an agent and less of a recipient of God's blessing. The good life does not drop out of the sky. It is fabricated in the human condition, the work of human hands.

Let me give another example of a shift in consciousness. Imagine the scene of the crucifixion. Jesus hangs on the cross. On either side of him, two felons are dying the same death. At the foot of the cross stand two figures, one his mother, the other the beloved disciple. Where do you put yourself in the picture? This picture represents one of the central mysteries of our faith, one that we re-enact in the celebration of the eucharist, the act of public worship of the believing community. As a girl growing up, there was only one place for me in that picture, only one woman in that scenario of sacrifice, of laying down your life in the service of others. Mary, the mother, stands at the foot of the cross weeping. The drama is played out in the figure of Christ on the cross. The good thief and the bad thief play their part. As a woman, I understood my role to be that of a bystander, full of sorrow but powerless to do anything. That was more or less the limit of my understanding until just a few years ago when I saw a piece of sculpture showing a woman's body, the arms outstretched, the face furrowed in pain, the body slumped in exhaustion. It was called the crucified woman. It broke open for me my whole understanding of redemption. Baptism in Christ is not just watching someone else act on my behalf. It is to become personally responsible and accountable for life and death, my own and that of others. The disciple, whether Mary or John, follows the master.

Every human being, female as well as male, has to choose as
did the good thief and the bad thief. The time comes when
each of us must die. But to be female in a male-dominated
Church is a handicap for the development of our faith. The
fact that faith has been handed down to us by a succession of
men speaking from the subjectivity of their own lives, but
rarely by women using our experience to name ·sin and
salvation, impedes our understanding of the gospel.

I am reminded of my friend Yvonne who sadly died of
breast cancer some six years ago. We were students of
theology together in Toronto and she pushed me to think
more critically about Scripture, about how we interpret it
and how the text is so often used to disempower women. We
belonged together to an ecumenical women's group that met
regularly. Yvonne was an Anglican. She had always
involved herself in parish catechetics and Anglican women's
organizations but time and again, she would find herself up
against the male clerical authority that blocked her sense of
where she wanted to develop the work she was doing. Each
time she accepted the message that her experience was
limited and that she lacked professional training. Each time
she sought a way out of the impasse by doing some further
training and then taking on another task. Only gradually did
she become aware of the underlying messages that women
must do as they are told, that women may not make
decisions that affect the life of the parish, that what women
do is unimportant anyway. By the time I met her, Yvonnne
was completing seminary training and was looking for a
bishop who would undertake to ordain her. In Canada in
1980, women were accepted as candidates for ordination.
The hurdles were the practical ones of placement. Yvonne
was finally accepted and a bishop did adopt her for
ordination, although as his diocese was not the one where
Yvonne was living, she would have had to move. But by that
time Yvonne had cancer and had had a mastectomy.

Newly out of hospital, she came to one of our women's
group meetings. We spent the evening talking about our
health, our hospital experiences and of course of how our

sense of self is wrapped up in our body image. We asked her to preside at the informal liturgy which always concluded our meeting. She took bread and broke it and said the words we say in memory of Jesus: "This is my body broken for you." As we ate that bread and passed the cup of wine, I was aware of a shift in consciousness, in my sense of self and sense of God. In that celebration of women, of women asking for physical healing, for health, for wholeness, presided over by a woman, the Body of Christ was suddenly a woman's body. Women's suffering and denigration was Christ's suffering and death. In a way not available to me before, I knew that God knows what it is to have a woman's body, what it is that women suffer. Jesus died for women. By seeing Christ as a woman, by saying God is a woman who suffers in her body, I could find new wealth of meaning in the knowledge that I am made in the image of God. By projecting my own experience and the collective experience of women onto God, I was released to know God more intimately. Equally I could the more confidently allow God to be other than myself, to be Other, inscrutable mystery. Conversely, of course, I realized that because we always use male language and images in Church, because the priesthood is visibly male, I had never really been fully in touch with the redemption and resurrection of women's bodies from our baptismal immersion in Christ.

I have tried to say three things. First, the better our self-awareness, the better we can know and love and serve our neighbour, the better we can speak of God. Second, the ideas and language and images we use to talk about God are always akin to the way we talk about ourselves. We project onto God from our human experience. We say God is like a father who is overjoyed to welcome home a son who has been far away for a long time. God is like a woman who can never forget the child of her womb. At the same time, the qualities and actions we have attributed to God become criteria for human conduct. We want to be god-like: good, holy, just, loving, forgiving. Third, just as we cannot know ourselves apart from the human community where history and geography have located us, no more can we know God. Learning about God is a community enterprise as well as a personal one. Our very culture is part of the language in which we express our understanding of God. Any shift in self-perception, in self consciousness, whether as individuals or as societies, will shift what we want to say about God. If we talk about God in new ways, we will discover new aspects to our self and to each other. We have all grown up with some idea of what a good person is, some idea of what it is to be a woman in society, some idea of what to expect of men. The idea, the imagination is just ahead, as it were, and we live up to it and into it. Sometimes living forces us to revise our ideas as we surely do in marriage or raising children. I have found that my ideas about being a person and a human being were very much in conflict with what was expected of me as a woman. Independence, leadership and authority are part of what is envisaged for a human being. But women, married with children, dependent on a husband's income, homemakers, are not treated as autonomous human persons in today's world. And in the Church, even more poignantly, the conflict has to be resolved between, on the one hand, Mary the image of the mother, the virgin, the disciple, the apostle and on the other, the lives of real women.

If we can say of God that there are three equal persons in the Godhead, creator, redeemer and sustainer, mutual in relationship, distinct in function yet living in unison, what do we then say of human relationships? I hope we can say that domination and subordination in relationship is not godlike. If our social and ecclesiastical arrangements are not good for women, then they are not good, not God-given. Women are brought up to submit to the power of men. Laity are expected to be ruled by a clerical hierarchy. In our experience these systems constitute bonds that enslave us, narrowing our choices, limiting our imagination, curtailing our development. But God is always revealed where people are set free, where women and men claim the fullness of humanity, where we laity identify ourselves as the People of God. Then the male and the clerical assume a proper proportion and a proper relation to the whole we call justice, the only ground in which love and peace may flourish.

From a talk given at St James's, Piccadilly in October 1986.

Appendix

Open Letter to the Bishop of London from the Dean of King's College London (KQC)

Support for the Ordination of Women from Different Churches and Traditions.

We care greatly for good relations between the Roman Catholic Church and the Church of England, as we care for good relations with all Churches. Whatever the short-term effects of introducing the ordination of women might be, in the long run we hope that the Roman Catholic Church could well benefit from the experience of seeing women ordained in the Church of England. Not surprisingly, we ourselves hold different views about the nature of the priesthood. Nonetheless, we wish the Church of England well in its endeavours to discover a fuller ministry of men and women in the service of God. We warmly commend the Dean of King's' paper for the attention of those concerned with this question and find ourselves in general agreement with him.

The Revd Dr Robert Butterworth, SJ
The Revd Dr Robert Murray, SJ
The Revd Prebendary Michael Saward
The Very Revd Alan Webster
The Rt Revd Kenneth Woollcombe

Dear Bishop,

You devoted your October and November newsletters to the subject of the ordination of women and put forward certain aspects of the issue that are not, you claimed, being faced at present. This is an attempt to consider these, and other aspects with the same serious and reasonable tone that you yourself employed.

O　　=　　Your objection
A　　=　　Answer

1. O.　Priests are ordained to the one Catholic Church of which the Church of England claims to be a part. At the Reformation the Church of England made a distinction between those aspects of its Faith and Orders which it had inherited from the past and which it was its duty to maintain, and those aspects it felt free to modify. The Church of England does not have the authority to alter anything which is the possession of the whole.

　　A.　It was a matter of dispute at the Reformation which aspects were to be maintained and which modified. For example, the Papacy argued that the universal primacy of the See of Peter was the possession of the whole. The Church of England disagreed. Many changes then made by the Church in England, which Rome at the time regarded as an illegitimate alteration of what belonged to the Church as a whole, have subsequently been accepted by her. If the ordination of women is in accord with the mind of Christ, it will in the course of time be recognized as such by other parts of the Catholic Church. If it is in accord with the mind of Christ, it would be a failure of the Church of England's own integrity to delay indefinitely pending agreement with the Church as a whole.

2. O.　A decision to ordain women would imply that the priesthood has been defective for nearly 2000 years.

　　A.　This implication is not necessary and would be unhistorical. As Newman argued, it is in the nature of the

Catholic Church to be open to change and development. Truths implicit in the deepest levels of the New Testament may take generations to be brought forward and affirmed, e.g. that slavery is contrary to the will of God. The Church is part of history and what is possible in one generation may not have been realizable before that time. What is essential is that theological development should be consonant with the teaching of holy scripture. The ordination of women is both consonant with scripture and is demanded by its central insights.

3. O. Christ chose only men as his Apostles. He did this deliberately and to question his action here is to question his authority in all matters.

A. The Eternal Son of God became a person at a particular place and time. He was not born in Athens in the 5th century BC or in New England in the 20th century AD. The redemption he wrought did not derive from what he knew but from what he did. He did not, for example, know the time of the end; but he did know how to be the Son of God incarnate. He lived out his perfect sonship, in the conditions of his time, shaped by its general outlook. He challenged that outlook when it conflicted with the clear will of God, e.g. on Sabbath observance. He challenged it by his treatment of women and by according them a share in his ministry. Should he have challenged it even more directly by making women apostles? The Apostles were called by Christ to leave their homes and to go out and about in the countryside calling men to repent before the imminent rule of God in human affairs. Given the position of women in society at that time, would it have been sensible to do this? Or even a real option to do so?

4. O. God made us male and female. This entails real differences in our psycho-sexual being and in our personal identity. Furthermore, we are to be saved *in* our masculinity and femininity, not from them. A female priesthood would blur and undermine the genuine diversity willed by God in both creation and redemption.

A.   It is important to distinguish between a) differences in personal characteristics, such as whether a person is fierce or gentle, b) differences in function, i.e. the function of childbearing which belongs to females and not to males, and c) the symbolic effect of performing certain roles.

a) There are certainly differences in personal characteristics between males and females which are to be respected and cherished. So, for example, in the case of the Diaconate, men and women bring different characteristics to their ministry, differences which reflect not only their personalities but their sex. This is part of the richness intended by God. No one wants a drab monotone Diaconate. The same is true of the priesthood.

b) There are no priestly functions that women are physically or psychologically incapable of performing.

c) Symbols are certainly important. For example, when a Chinese person becomes ordained in a European context, this is a sign of the universality of the Church. You, however, argue that there is an intrinsic connection between maleness and priesthood so that a woman ordained would be a false or misleading symbol. This point is considered in paragraph 6.

5. O.   God chose to become incarnate as a male person. As parents might speak to young children in a way that adapts to their needs, so God, though himself above gender, told us to address him as Father and was incarnate as male.

A.   God did indeed choose to become incarnate as a man. For good reason, for it is God's reason. But that reason is not known to us. We can only speculate. The most obvious explanation has, again, to do with the place of woman in ancient patriarchal societies. Though both Old and New Testaments tell us of women exercising a *prophetic* ministry, the association of female "priesthood" in the ancient world made this idea unacceptable in the early Church, while the fact that we do not hear of the fulness of apostolic ministry being exercised by women in the early Church can be accounted for by contemporary assumptions about social roles.

What is now unthinkable to some, God incarnate as a woman, was, in the light of what God wanted to reveal, unthinkable in the circumstances at that time. God has indeed chosen to reveal himself to us in terms of our understanding, first by making a womb and cradle of Hebrew culture and then by being born in it. But his incarnation is adapted to our humanity and our culture, not primarily our sexuality.

Given that God was incarnate as a male person, what are the implications of this? It does not prevent women from becoming saints and mystics. It does not prevent them becoming spiritual directors and Abbesses. It does not prevent them becoming Christians and witnessing to Christ through secular employment or full-time ministry in the Church. Why should it prevent them becoming ordained as a presbyter or priest in the Church of God? Is there a symbolic effect about a woman priest that militates against a true grasp of the incarnation?

6. O. In human life the masculine is associated with giving and the female with receiving. God is pre-eminently the giver, who takes the initiative for our salvation. A male priesthood symbolizes the initiative, as well as the authority, of God. Mary, on the other hand, symbolizes the receptive, obedient response which is due from mankind.

A. It seems dangerous to associate a giving and receiving type of love exclusively with either masculinity or femininity. For many, if not most, people the giving of love *par excellence* is known in the love of a mother.

God is indeed the one who takes the initiative and the Son of God was born as a man. But it would of course be circular to argue from this that only masculine love should be associated with taking the initiative.

Within the Blessed Trinity there is perfect mutual giving and receiving between the Father and Son. It was this Eternal relationship that was disclosed in human terms. In the Gospels the Son owes all that he has, and receives all that he is and does, from the Father to whom he seeks to be perfectly responsive. The picture we have at the Baptism of Christ is the truth of the whole incarnate story and this is the story in time of what happens endlessly in the Godhead. It is not therefore simply Mary who is a symbol of human responsiveness to the Father but Christ himself. Indeed, ontologically, her responsiveness is grounded in and derived from the perfect filial response of Christ to his Father. For Christ is the exemplar and symbol of receiving (as well as giving) love. This, too, should be symbolized by those who share in his priesthood.

The priesthood represents not only the initiative and authority of God but the receptivity and obedience of mankind. As Christ, the true priest, unites in himself both giving and receiving, so those who partake of his priesthood symbolize both aspects of the love of the Godhead. It is no more tenable to argue for an all male priesthood than it would be to argue for an all female one.

Symbols are certainly important and the ordination of women to the priesthood would have a profoundly positive effect. It would bring home the truth that in Christ ''there is neither male nor female'' (Galatians 3.28), or to put it another way, that God includes within himself the fullness of masculinity and femininity. Further, it would help to communicate more of this feminine side of divine love.

7. If this reasoning is sound, there is no theological reason why women should not be ordained. And there are two vital reasons why they should be. Firstly, many women feel an *Internum testimonium Spiritus Sancti* leading them to offer themselves for ordination. The Church should now test this, in individual cases, as it does for men. If there is no theological reason why women should not be ordained, as has been argued, the present failure to test women's vocation is an act of basic injustice at the heart of the Church's ministry. Secondly, the priesthood would be greatly enriched both by the feminine qualities which women would bring to it and by the symbolic effect mentioned above. This would, in the course of time, lead

to a much healthier balance between men and women in the Church as a whole.

Yours sincerely,

Richard

The Reverend Richard Harries